SHARḤ AL-WARAQĀT

Al-Waraqāt fī Uṣūl al-Fiqh

IMĀM AL-JUWAYNĪ

SHARḤ AL-WARAQĀT

Al-Waraqāt fī Uṣūl al-Fiqh
IMĀM AL-JUWAYNĪ

With brief commentary
JALĀL AL-DĪN AL-MAḤALLĪ

Translation & Notes by
MUSA FURBER

SHARḤ AL-WARAQĀT: AL-MAḤALLĪ'S NOTES ON IMĀM AL-JUWAYNĪ'S ISLAMIC JURISPRUDENCE PAMPHLET

ISBN 978-0-9858840-4-8 (paper)
ISBN: 978-0-9858840-5-5 (EPUB, *Al-Waraqāt* only)

Published by: Islamosaic (publications@islamosaic.com)

بسم الله الرحمن الرحيم

All praise is to Allah alone, the Lord of the Worlds
And may He send His benedictions upon
our master Muhammad, his Kin
and his Companions
and grant them
peace

TRANSLITERATION KEY

ء	ʼ[1]	ر	r[6]	ف	f
ا	ā, a	ز	z	ق	q[13]
ب	b	س	s	ك	k
ت	t	ش	sh	ل	l
ث	th[2]	ص	ṣ[7]	م	m
ج	j	ض	ḍ[8]	ن	n
ح	ḥ[3]	ط	ṭ[9]	ه	h[14]
خ	kh[4]	ظ	ẓ[10]	و	ū, u, w
د	d	ع	ʻ[11]	ي	ī, i, y
ذ	dh[5]	غ	gh[12]		

1. A distinctive glottal stop made at the bottom of the throat. It is also used to indicate the running of two words into one, e.g., *bismi'Llāh*.
2. Pronounced like the *th* in *think*.
3. Hard *h* sound made at the Adam's apple in the middle of the throat.
4. Pronounced like *ch* in Scottish *loch*.
5. Pronounced like *th* in *this*.
6. A slightly trilled *r* made behind the upper front teeth.
7. An emphatic *s* pronounced behind the upper front teeth.
8. An emphatic *d*-like sound made by pressing the entire tongue against the upper palate.
9. An emphatic *t* sound produced behind the front teeth.
10. An emphatic *th* sound, like the *th* in *this*, made behind the front teeth.
11. A distinctive Semitic sound made in the middle throat and sounding to a Western ear more like a vowel than a consonant.
12. A guttural sound made at the top of the throat resembling the untrilled German and French *r*.
13. A hard *k* sound produced at the back of the palate.
14. This sound is like the English *h* but has more body. It is made at the very bottom of the throat and pronounced at the beginning, middle, and end of words.

CONTENTS

المحتويات

TRANSLITERATION KEY VII

TRANSLATOR'S PREFACE VIII

1 AUTHOR'S INTRODUCTION 1

2 Categories of Phrases 12

3 Commands 17

4 Universal and Particular Applicability 23

5 Ambiguity & Clarification 30

6 Actions of the Prophet ﷺ 32

7 Abrogation 35

8 Conflicting Evidence 42

9 Scholarly Consensus 48

10 Declarative Statements and Reports 51

11 Analogical Reasoning 56

12 Prohibition and Permissibility 61

13 Presumption of Continuity 63

14 Order of Precedence in Which Evidence is Cited 65

15 The Mufti, His Petitioner, and Emulation 67

16 Personal Reasoning 71

BASIC TEXT OF THE ENGLISH TRANSLATION 74

BIBLIOGRAPHY 92

ABOUT THE TRANSLATOR 94

TRANSLATOR'S PREFACE

مقدّمة المترجم

In the Name of God, Most Merciful and Compassionate

KNOWLEDGE OF THE LEGAL STATUS and performance of actions is the subject of the discipline of law (*fiqh*). How this knowledge is known is the subject of jurisprudence (*uṣūl al-fiqh*).

The English phrase "Islamic law" refers to the subject known in Arabic as "*fiqh*." The original meaning of "*fiqh*" in Arabic relates to deep understanding. Imam al-Ghazālī and others note that the early generations used the term "*fiqh*" to refer to knowledge of the path to the Afterlife, knowing the subtle vitiations of the tongue, spoilers of deeds, having strong comprehension as to the paltriness of this life, intense desire for the bounties of the Afterlife, and fear being dominant in the heart. Later, the term settled on the definition we have now: "knowledge of the legal rulings associated with deeds, obtained through specific evidences." A scholar of *fiqh* is known as a *faqīh* (pl. *fuqahā*).

The English phrases "Islamic legal methodology," "foundations of Islamic law," "Islamic jurisprudence," and the like, refer to the subject known in Arabic as *uṣūl al-fiqh*, which is defined as "knowing the general evidences of *fiqh*, how to use them, and the conditions for the person using them." A scholar of *uṣūl al-fiqh* is known as an *uṣūlī* (pl. *uṣūliyyūn*). The proper exercise of *uṣūl al-fiqh* is *ijtihād* – exercising expert reasoning.

The linguistic meaning of *ijtihād* is "expending all efforts and energy while seeking a matter in order to reach it to its furthest extent," and its meaning according to the scholars of the methods of jurisprudence is not far from this: "the jurist expending all efforts to obtain a legal ruling through legal deduction." Both meanings indicate that those who perform it must expend all possible efforts to arrive at their answer.

Evidence for the exercise of *ijtihād* comes from the prophetic report that

> When the Messenger of Allah ﷺ sent Mu'ādh ibn Jabal to Yemen, he asked: "What will you do if a matter is referred to you for judgement?" Mu'ādh said: "I will judge according to the Book of Allah." The Prophet asked: "What if you find no solution in the Book of Allah?" Mu'ādh said: "Then I will judge by the Sunnah of the Prophet." The Prophet asked: "And what if you do not find it in the Sunnah of the Prophet?" Mu'ādh said: "Then I will make *ijtihād* to formulate my own judgement." The Prophet patted Mu'ādh's chest and said "Praise be to Allah who has guided the messenger of His Prophet to that which pleases Him and His Prophet."[1]

Someone who is qualified to perform *ijtihād* is known as a *mujtahid*.

Classical books of jurisprudence mention in detail the knowledge and skills which are required for *ijtihād*, in addition to the etiquette one should observe when carrying it out. These requirements and etiquette set standards not only for an answer being acceptable to follow, but also serve to ensure that the application of these knowledge and skills results in sound judgments and minimizes the potential for errors. So just as the rules of grammar protect those who follow them from mistakes in expressions, the rules of logic protect those who follow them from mistakes in arguments; jurisprudence sets standards for interpreting legal texts and making legal arguments which, when followed correctly, protect from making mistakes in arriving at legal rulings. In short: correct methodology and its sound application by an individual with the proper credentials and etiquette lead to fewer errors.

---

1 Abū Dāwūd (3594).

In summary, Islamic jurisprudence boils down to three things: knowing the general evidences, how to use them, and the conditions for the person using them. Or, stated more abstractly: sources of law, methodology of research and interpretation, and the researcher. Its immediate benefit is helping to reduce the role of subjectivity and errors in discovering legal rulings.

Paradigms of Islamic Jurisprudence

Imām al-Shāfiʿī is credited with being the first person to write about the subject of Islamic jurisprudence. The Imām passed away in 204 AH, so one might ask whether earlier scholars operated without jurisprudence; and, if they did, why they did not write it down. Something to keep in mind is that the *mujtahid*s – starting with the Companions (may God be pleased with them all) – had some method that they followed, even if it was not explicit. While one or a few Imāms may be given credit with being the first to record Islamic jurisprudence and *fiqh*, this does not mean that their predecessors were in any way deficient in these disciplines. There were many other participants sharing in this endeavor. Writing books was just one of many ways scholars participated. One of the greatest Imāms was asked why he did not author any books. His response was that he authored students.

Historically, there were two basic paradigms for approaching Islamic jurisprudence. The first is the way of the theologians (*ṭarīqat al-mutakallimīn*). This is the paradigm followed by the Shāfiʿī, Māliki, and Ḥanbalī schools of law. According to this paradigm, principles are first set down and these principles are used to find legal rulings. The second paradigm is the way of the jurists (*ṭarīqat al-fuqahā'*). This is the paradigm followed by the Ḥanafī school of law. According to this paradigm, principles for how the school's eponymous Imām arrived at legal rulings are derived by examining his legal judgments.

Later, a third paradigm developed which involves synthesizing the first two. A fourth style of jurisprudence literature involves mentioning basic principles, each with the differences between schools, and then building legal rulings based upon the principles.

The classical way of teaching and writing *uṣūl al-fiqh* is to mention the four agreed-upon sources (Quran, Sunnah, consensus, legal analogy); then it mentions the evidences which are disputed by some, including the singular opinion of a Companion, custom, revealed legislation from before Islam, juridical preference, presumption of continuity, unrestricted interests; and then the conditions for the *mujtahid*.

A recent development in jurisprudence literature collects the same issues but in the order their need would occur to someone trying to discover Islamic legal rulings. A jurist begins by asking what is a ruling, and then progresses through the questions concerning authoritative evidence, authenticating individual evidence, what individual specimens of evidence mean, and so on. This approach exposes the challenges faced in the earliest generations by people working with Islamic sources, and gives us insight into how and why they made their decisions.

Studying Jurisprudence

Students of jurisprudence read through a series of texts with their instructors. The first text usually reads like a list of definitions and rules, with occasional examples. Each book in the series adds more definitions, rules, and examples – as well as variant opinions, and argumentation to champion one opinion.

One of the first books of jurisprudence taught to students is the *Waraqāt* of Imām al-Juwaynī (d. 468 AH). The text is limited to definitions and rules – with very few examples and explanations – making it a perfect book for memorizing the very basics. But it requires a commentary, so it is often taught with a short interlinear commentary by Jalāl al-Dīn al-Maḥallī (d. 864 AH). Al-Maḥallī's commentary fleshes out the basic text with explanations, arguments behind its opinions, and numerous examples. The commentary has several derivative works for students interested in something more expansive. One of the better known derivatives is Ibn Qāsim 'Abādī's interlinear commentary which covers each word of al-Maḥallī's commentary. Two less-known derivatives are meta-commentaries by Aḥmad bin Muḥammad al-Dimyāṭī and by Aḥmad bin ʿAbd al-Khaṭīb al-Jāwī. Both of them draw on material from Ibn Qāsim and other sources. (For comparison, these last two books, printed on same-sized paper, are 24 pages and 184 pages, respectively.) In addition to al-Maḥallī's commentary and its derivatives, there is also the commentary of an earlier scholar Ibn Firkāh (d. 690 AH), which is thorough, detailed, and lucid.

This translation is an English rendering of Imām al-Juwaynī's *Waraqāt* with Jalāl al-Dīn al-Maḥallī's complete interlinear commentary. The Arabic text from *Waraqāt* and al-Maḥallī's commentary are included. Instead of bringing it all at the beginning of each section, I have tried to break it up into the chunks that are likely to be taught together.

Introduction to the Translation

The translation of al-Maḥallī's commentary was done over a few weeks during January 2004, sometime soon after completing the translation of Abū Shujāʿ al-Aṣfahānī's *Matn al-Ghāyat wa al-Taqrīb.*

There are a few things the reader should know in order to derive the greatest benefit from this translation. Printed Arabic has its own conventions for presenting basic texts with the various forms of commentaries. One of the most common conventions is to place a basic text between parentheses, with commentary outside the parenthesis. Additionally, the page is sometimes divided so that different texts occupy different spaces of the page. These conventions seem suitable for the Arabic script – especially for texts which use punctuation sparsely (if at all). After looking at various ways to present the content of this translation which consists of a basic text, a complete interlinear commentary, and a few notes from other works, I decided to follow the following conventions:

- The basic text, Imām al-Juwaynī's *Waraqāt*, will appear in **bold**.
- The commentary, by Jalāl al-Dīn al-Maḥallī, will appear as normal, plain text.

Comments from additional sources will be enclosed within parenthesis, with an indication of their origin:

- (Ibn Qāsim: ...) – for notes from Ibn Qāsim's meta-commentary
- (trans.: ...) – for notes from the translator
- Examples are introduced with *Example* (or a similar label).

When a particular portion of a quotation is of particular significance, it is indicated according to the preceding example.

One of the requirements of an Arabic interlinear commentary is that the comments are introduced without breaking the syntax of the original. I have tried to follow this in my translation, sometimes prompting me to deviate from superior writing style. There are occasions where the commentary includes a quotation and the final punctuation is placed after the quotation mark as it is needed by the basic text.

It is my hope that this translation serves English-speaking audiences as an introduction to the basic topics of jurisprudence and puts them on their way to studying more advanced material. Students will benefit most if they read the book with a qualified instructor – after first studying a basic work of *fiqh*.

The people who helped me with this project are too numerous to mention. I owe a great debt to the Shāfi'ī sheikhs with whom I had the honor to study this subject, including Sheikhs Muṣṭafā al-Turkmāni, 'Abd al-Qādir al-Khaṭīb, Ali Gomaa, and most of all: Sheikhs Ḥusayn Darwīsh and Muḥammad Ṣulṭān Jād. Students further along with their studies reviewed drafts of the translation and offered innumerable corrections, encouragement, and advice. Several merit special mention for their generous help with editing and reviewing the text throughout its various stages: Talal al-Azam, Omar Qureshi, Jawad Qureshi, Nuri Friedlander, and Edgar Hopida. Last but not least, I owe much to my wife and children for their constant support and sacrifice throughout the years.

May God reward the authors of this work and the people they mentioned therein. May God grant all who have been mentioned in this preface – and us – His mercy, and may He make us among those who benefit from this noble text. Where I have succeeded, it is only through the grace of Allāh; where I have faltered it is from my own shortcomings.

Musa Furber
Abu Dhabi
August 30, 2013

AUTHOR'S INTRODUCTION

المقدّمة

بسم الله الرحمن الرحيم

الحمد لله رب العالمين والصلاة على سيد المرسلين محمد وعلى آله وصحبه وسلم وبعد. (هذه ورقات قليلة تشتمل على معرفة فصول من أصول الفقه) ينتفع بها المبتدئ وغيره.

In the name of God, the Merciful and Compassionate

All praise is to Allah, Lord of the worlds. May blessings be upon the best of the Messengers our leigelord Muḥammad, and upon his household and companions, and peace.

To commence: **These** few **pages include some of the topics of jurisprudence** which will benefit beginners and others.

The Meanings Of "base," "branch," and "understanding"

(فصل) (وذلكَ) أي لفظ أصول الفقه (مؤلّفٌ من جزءين) [أحدهما أصول والآخر الفقه] (مُفْرَدَيْنِ) من الإفراد مقابل التركيب لا التثنية والجمع، والمؤلف يعرف بمعرفة ما ألف منه.

This – the phrase "bases of law" [in Arabic: *uṣūl al-fiqh*] – **is composed of two individual components** – from "component" in contrast to "composition," not [from the word "singular" in contrast to] "plurality." Compositions are understood by knowing their components.

(فالأصلُ) الذي هو [مفرد الجزء] الأول (ما يبنى عليه غيره، والفرع ما بُنى على غيره) [كأصل الجدار أي أساسه وأصل الشجرة أي طرفها الثابت في الأرض]. [والفرع الذي هو مقابل الأصل ما يبنى على غيره] كفروع الشجرة لأصلها وفروع الفقه لأصوله.

The word "base" [***aṣl***], the singular of the first component, **is a thing upon which another thing is built.** *Example:* the *base of a wall*, meaning its foundation; and the *base of a tree*, meaning its extremity which is firmly fixed in the ground.

The word "branch" [***far'***] – which is in contrast to "base" – **is a thing that is built upon another thing.** *Example:* a tree's branches in relationship to its base, and the branches of *fiqh* in relationship to its bases.

(والفقهُ) الذي هو الجزء الثاني، له معنى لغوي وهو الفهم، ومعنى شرعي وهو (معرفةُ الأحكامِ الشّرعيةِ الّتي طريقُها الاجتهادُ) كالعلم بأن النية في الوضوء واجبة، وأن الوتر مندوب، وأن النية من الليل شرط في صوم رمضان، وأن الزكاة واجبة في مال الصبي، وغير واجبة في الحلي المباح، وأن القتل بمثقل يوجب القصاص، ونحو ذلك من مسائل الخلاف، بخلاف ما ليس طريقه الاجتهاد، كالعلم بأن الصلوات الخمس واجبة، وأن الزنا محرم، ونحو ذلك من المسائل القطعية فلا يسمى فقهاً.

The word "law" [*fiqh*] is its second component. It has a linguistic meaning (understanding); and it has a legal meaning: **knowing legal rulings which are reached through *ijtihād* [qualified reasoning].**

[*Fiqh* is] knowing that, for example, intention during ablution is obligatory, Witr Prayer is recommended, making intention at night is a condition for fasting [each day of] Ramadan, *zakāt* is an obligation for the property of youths but not an obligation for lawful jewelry, murder with a blunt instrument renders reciprocal punishment obligatory, and similar issues that are open to differences of opinion. This [*fiqh*] is contrary to things that are not known through *ijtihād*, such as knowing that the five prayers are obligatory, that fornication is unlawful, and similar issues which are certain [*qaṭʿī*] – since knowing these issues is not called "*fiqh*."

فالمعرفة هنا العلم بمعنى الظن.

Here the word "knowing" [*maʿrifa*] means "knowledge" [*ʿilm*], with the same meaning as "probable" [*ẓann*].

Categories of Rulings

(فصل) (والأحكامُ) المرادة فيها ذكر (سبعةٌ: الواجب، والمندوب، والمباح، والمحظور، والمكروه، والصحيح، والباطل)

فالفقه العلم بالواجب والمندوب إلى آخر السبعة. أي بأن هذا الفعل واجب [وهذا مندوب] وهذا مباح وهكذا إلى آخر جزيئات السبعة.

There are seven rulings:

1. **Obligation [*wājib*]**
2. **Recommended [*mandūb*]**
3. **Neutral [*mubāḥ*]**

4. **Forbidden [*maḥẓūr*]**
5. **Offensive [*makrūh*]**
6. **Valid [*ṣaḥīḥ*]**
7. **Invalid [*bāṭil*]**

Hence, "*fiqh*" is knowledge of the obligatory, recommended, and so on to the end of these seven. That is: knowledge that this action is obligatory, this action is recommended, this action is merely permissible, and so on until the end of the seven.

(فالواجبُ) من حيث وصفه بالوجوب: (ما يُثابُ على فعله، ويُعاقبُ على تَرْكه.)
ويكفي في صدق العقاب وجوده لواحد من العصاة مع العفو عن غيره.
ويجوز أن يريد ويترتب العقاب على تركه كما عبر به غيره فلا ينافي العفو.
(والمندوبُ) من حيث وصفه بالندب: (ما يثاب على فعله، ولا يعاقب على تركه.)
(والمُبَاحُ) من حيث وصفه بالإباحة: (ما لا يثاب على فعله، ولا يعاقب على تركه.)
أي ما لا يتعلق بكل من فعله وتركه ثواب ولا عقاب.
(والمَحْظور) من حيث وصفه بالحظر أي الحرمةُ: (ما يثاب على تركه) امتثالًا، (ويعاقب على فعله.) [ويكفي في صدق العقاب وجوده لواحد من العصاة مع العفو عن غيره. ويجوز أن يريد ويترتب العقاب على فعله كما عبر به غيره فلا ينافي العفو].
(والمَكْروهُ) من حيث وصفه بالكراهة: (ما يثاب على تركه) امتثالًا، (ولا يعاقب على فعله.)

Obligation (in that it is described with being obligatory) **is anything for which one is rewarded if performed and punished if omitted.** In order for punishment to hold true, it suffices that one of the disobedient is punished even though all others are forgiven. [The author] might also have meant that "punishment is a consequence of its omission" – as other scholars have expressed it – so it does not negate forgiveness.

Recommended (in that it is described with being commended) **is anything for which one is rewarded for if performed, yet not punished if omitted.**

Neutral (in that it is described with permissibility) **is anything for which one is neither rewarded for if performed** or omitted**, nor punished for if omitted** or performed. Thus, both its performance and omission are not associated with reward or punishment.

Forbidden (in that it is described with being forbidden, meaning prohibition) **is anything for which one is rewarded if omitted,** out of compliance, **and punished if performed.** In order for punishment to hold true, it suffices that one of the disobedient is punished even though all others are forgiven. [The author] might also have meant that "punishment is a consequence of its performance" – as other scholars have expressed it – so it does not negate forgiveness.

Offensive (in that it is described with offensiveness) **is anything for which one is rewarded if omitted**, out of compliance, **yet not punished if performed.**

(والصَّحيحُ) من حيث وصفه بالصحة: (ما يتعلَّقُ به النّفوذُ ويُعتدُّ به) بأن استجمع ما يعتبر فيه شرعاً، عقداً كان أو عبادة.

(والباطلُ) من حيث وصفه بالبطلان: (ما لا يتعلّق به النّفوذُ ولا يُعتدُّ به) بأن لم يستجمع ما يعتبر فيه شرعاً، عقداً كان أو عبادة.

والعقد يتصف بالنفوذ والاعتداد.

والعبادة تتصف بالاعتداد فقط اصطلاحاً .

Valid (in that it is described with validity) **is that to which being**

effective (trans.: in obtaining its intended purposes, such as permissibility of making use of in sales contract, or permissibility of intimate behavior in a marriage contract) **and of legal significance pertain**, by combining all matters of legal concern, whether [describing] a contract or an act of worship.

Invalid (in that it is described with invalidity) **is that to which being effective and of legal significance do not pertain**, by it failing to combine all matters of legal concern, whether [describing] a contract or an act of worship.

Contracts are described with being effective and of legal significance.

Worship is described as being of legal significance, only, in the technical sense.

Clarifying the meanings of knowledge, suspicion, and doubt

(فصل) (والفقه) بالمعنى الشرعي (أَخَصُّ من العلم) لصدق العلم بالنحو وغيره، فكل فقه علم، وليس كل علم فقهاً.

(والعِلْمُ معرفةُ المعلومِ) أي إدراك ما من شأنه أن يعلم (على ما هو به في الواقع) كإدراك الإنسان بأنه حيوان ناطق.

(والجَهْلُ تصوُّرُ الشيء) أي إدراكه (على خلاف ما هو في الواقع) كإدراك الفلاسفة أن العالم وهو ما سوى الله تعالى قديم. وبعضهم وصف هذا الجهل بالمركب، وجعل البسيط عدم العلم بالشيء، كعدم علمنا بما تحت الأرضين، وبما في بطون البحار. وعلى ما ذكره المصنف لا يسمى هذا جهلاً.

Fiqh – in the legal sense – **is more constrained than knowledge** [***'ilm***], since *'ilm* holds true when pertaining to grammar and other things, as all understanding is knowledge, but not all knowledge is understanding. **The word "*'ilm*" [means] knowing that which is known** (i.e., perceiving that which by its nature is known) **as it is in reality.** *Example:* A human perceiving that he is a sentient animal.

Ignorance [*jahl*] is conceptualizing something (i.e., perceiving it) **contrary to as it is in reality.** *Example:* A philosopher perceiving that the world – which is everything other than God – is without beginning. Some have labeled this kind of ignorance as "compound [ignorance]," and defined "simple [ignorance]" as an [absolute] absence of knowledge concerning something, such as our absence of knowledge of what lies beneath the earth and in the depths of the seas. But according to what the author mentioned, this [simple ignorance] is not considered ignorance.

(والعلمُ الضّروريُّ ما لا يقعُ عن نظرٍ واستدلالٍ) كالعلم الواقع بإحدى الحواس الخمس الظاهرة، وهي السمع والبصر واللمس والشم والذوق فإنه يحصل بمجرد الإحساس بها من غير نظر واستدلال.

(وأمّا العلمُ المُكْتَسَبُ فهو الموقوفُ على النّظر والاستدلال) كالعلم بأن العالم حادث، فإنه موقوف على النظر في العالم وما نشاهده فيه من التغير، فينتقل من تغيره إلى حدوثه.

Compulsory knowledge [*al-'ilm al-ḍarūrī*] is that which does not depend on pondering and inference. *Example:* knowledge taking place through one of the five outward senses – hearing, sight, touch, smell, and taste – since knowledge occurs simply by its sensation and without pondering [*naẓr*] and inference.

Acquired knowledge [*al-'ilm al-muktasab*] depends on pondering and inference. *Example:* Knowing that the world is created. This is because knowing this is dependent on contemplating the world and the changes we observe therein, and then deducing from its changes its having been created.

(والنّظر: هو الفكرُ في المنظور فيه) ليؤدي إلى المطلوب.

(والاستدلالُ: طَلَبُ الدّليل) ليؤدي إلى المطلوب فمؤدى النظر والاستدلال واحد فجمع المصنف بينهما في الإثبات والنفي تأكيداً.

(والدّليلُ: هو المرشِدُ إلى المطلوب) لأنه علامة عليه.

(والظّنُّ: تجويزُ أمرَيْنِ، أحدُهما أَظْهَرُ من الآخر) عند المجوز.

(والشّكُّ: تجويزُ أمرين، لا مزيّةَ لأحدهما على الآخر) عند المجوز، فالتردد في قيام زيد ونفيه على السواء شك، ومع رجحان الثبوت أو الانتفاء ظن.

Pondering [*naẓr*] is contemplating the state of the object of contemplation in order to lead to what is sought.

Inference [*istidlāl*] is seeking evidence [*al-dalīl*] in order to lead to what is sought. Hence, pondering and inference lead to the same thing.

Evidence [*al-dalīl*] is what guides to what is being sought, since it is its indicator.

Probable [*ẓann*] is when two matters are possible, with one being more apparent than the other, according to the beholder.

Doubt [*shakk*] is when two matters are possible, while neither possesses a feature distinguishing it over the other.

So, when the indecision concerning [the assertion that] Zayd is standing and its negation is equal, it is *doubt*. When its assertion or negation is preponderant, then it is *probable*.

The Meaning of Jurisprudence

(فصل) (وأصولُ الفقه) الذي وضع فيه هذه الورقات: (طرقُهُ) أي طرق الفقه، (على سبيل الإجمال) كمطلق الأمر والنهي وفعل النبي ﷺ والإجماع والقياس والاستصحاب، من حيث البحث عن أولها بأنه للوجوب والثاني بأنه للحرمة والباقي بأنها حجج وغير ذلك مما سيأتي مع ما يتعلق به بخلاف طرقه على سبيل التفصيل نحو ﴿وَأَقِيمُوا الصَّلَاةَ﴾ ﴿وَلَا تَقْرَبُوا الزِّنَا﴾ وصلاته ﷺ في الكعبة كما أخرجه الشيخان، والإجماع على أن لبنت الابن السدس مع بنت الصلب حيث لا عاصب لهما. وقياس الأرز على البر في امتناع بيع بعضه ببعض، إلا مثلاً بمثل يداً بيد، كما رواه مسلم. واستصحاب الطهارة لمن شك في بقائها، فليست من أصول الفقه وإن ذكر بعضها في كتبه تمثيلاً.

The bases of law [*uṣūl al-fiqh*] – which are the subject of these papers – **are its ways** (i.e., the ways of *fiqh*), **in general**. That is:

1. commands;
2. prohibitions;
3. actions of the Prophet ﷺ;
4. consensus;
5. analogical reasoning; and
6. the presumption of continuity

– in that it leads to knowing that the first is for obligation, the second for prohibition, that the rest are proofs, and other things that are forthcoming – along with what is associated with them.

This is in contrast to individual specimens of those general ways, such as:

1. *Establish the prayer* (Quran, 17:78).
2. *Do not approach illegal sexual relationships* (Quran, 17:32).
3. That he ﷺ prayed inside the Ka'ba as was transmitted in

Bukhārī and Muslim.[1]

4. The consensus that the filial granddaughter of the deceased is entitled to one-sixth [of the inheritance] when the deceased's daughter is alive provided that neither is accompanied by a universal inheritor.
5. The analogy that rice is similar to wheat with respect to the prohibition of transactions where it is both the item sold and its barter, unless they are identical and the transaction is final.[2]
6. Presuming the continuity of ritual purity for one who doubts its continuation.

These are not part of the bases of jurisprudence, even if they are mentioned in its books as examples.

(وكيفيّةُ الاستدلالِ بها) أي بطرق الفقه من حيث تفصيلها عند تعارضها لكونها ظنية من تقديم الخاص على العام والمقيد على المطلق وغير ذلك.

وكيفية الاستدلال بها تجر إلى صفات من يستدل بها وهو المجتهد.

فهذه الثلاثة هي الفن المسمى بأصول الفقه لتوقف الفقه عليه.

[The bases of law include the above] **and the manner in which they are used for inference.** That is: the ways the bases of *fiqh* are used for inference, from the perspective of using instances of evidence when they conflict (as they are probabilistic), such as giving precedence to the particular over the universal, the qualified over the categorical, and others.

The way in which they are used for inference leads to the characteristics of the one who uses them for inference: the *mujtahid.*

These three (Ibn Qāsim: i.e., the abstract ways of fiqh, how they are used for inference, and the characteristics of the *mujtahid*) are the discipline

1 Bukhārī (397, 1167, 1598–9), Muslim (1329).
2 Muslim (1587).

named "bases of jurisprudence" since *fiqh* depends upon them.

The Topics of Jurisprudence

(باب) (وأبوابُ أصولِ الفقهِ: أقسامُ الكلامِ، والأمرُ والنّهي، والعامّ والخاصّ،) ويذكر فيه المطلق والمقيد (والمجمل والمبيّن، [والنّصّ] والظّاهر،) وفي بعض النسخ والمؤول وسيأتي (والأفعال، والنّاسخ والمنسوخ، والإجماع، والأخبار، والقياس، والحظر والإباحة، وترتيب الأدلّة، وصفة المفتي والمستفتي، وأحكامُ المجتهدين.)

The topics of jurisprudence are:

- **Categories of phrases [*aqsām al-kalām*].**
- **Commands and prohibitions [*al-amr wa al-nahī*].**
- **Universal and particular applicability [*al-'āmm wa al-khāṣṣ*]** – wherein unqualified and qualified phrases [*al-muṭlaq wa al-muqayyad*] are mentioned.
- **Ambiguity and clarification [*al-mujmal wa al-mubayyan*].**
- **Evident [*al-ẓāhir*]** – and in some versions of the book: "interpreted significance" [*al-mu'awwal*] (which will come).
- **Actions of the Prophet ﷺ [*al-af'āl*].**
- **The abrogating and the abrogated [*al-nāsikh wa al-mansūkh*].**
- **Scholarly consensus [*al-ijma'*].**
- **Declarative statements and reports [*al-akhbār*].**
- **Analogical reasoning [*al-qiyās*].**
- **Prohibition and permissibility [*al-ḥaẓr wa al-ibāḥah*].**
- **The order of precedence in which evidence is cited [*tartīb al-adillah*].**
- **The attributes of those who give legal edicts and their petitioners [*ṣifāt al-muftī wa al-mustaftī*].**
- **Rulings pertaining to personal reasoning [*aḥkām al-mujtahidīn*].**

2

CATEGORIES OF PHRASES

أقسام الكلام

(فصل) (فأمّا أقسامُ الكلام فأقلّ ما يتركّبُ منه الكلام اسمان) نحو زيد قائم، (أو اسمٌ وفعلٌ) نحو قام زيد، (أو فعلٌ وحرفٌ) نحو ما قام، أثبته بعضهم ولم يعد الضمير في قام الراجع إلى زيد مثلاً لعدم ظهوره. والجمهور على عدِّه كلمة، (أو اسمٌ وحرفٌ) وذلك في النداء نحو يا زيد وإن كان المعنى أدعو أو أنادي زيداً.

(والكلامُ ينقسمُ إلى أمر ونهي) نحو قم ولا تقعد، (وخبر) نحو جاء زيد (واستخبار) وهو الاستفهام نحو هل قام زيد؟ فيقال: نعم أو لا.

(وينقسم أيضًا إلى تمنٍّ) نحو ليت الشباب يعود (وعَرْضٍ) نحو ألا تنزل عندنا (وقَسَمٍ) نحو والله لأفعلن كذا.

The bare minimums from which a phrase can be composed are:

1. **Two nouns.** *Example: Zayd qā'im*, "Zayd [is] standing."
2. **One noun and one verb.** *Example: Qām Zayd*, "Zayd stood."
3. **One verb and one particle.** *Example: Mā qām*, "[Zayd] didn't stand." Some scholars affirmed it and did not count the pronoun in *qām* which refers back (in this example) to "Zayd" due to its lack of visibility. However, the majority consider it a single word.
4. **One noun and one particle.** This is with vocatives, such as: *Yā Zayd!*, "O, Zayd!," even though the meaning is "I call..." – or: "I invoke..." – "...Zayd!"

Phrases divide into:

1. **Commands and prohibitions.** *Example:* "Stand!" and "Don't sit!"
2. **Declaratives.** *Example:* "Zayd came."
3. **Interrogatives** – which is soliciting information (e.g., "Did Zayd stand?"), that is answered with "yes" or "no".

Phrases also divide into:

1. **Fancy [*tamanin*].** *Example:* "If only youth would one day return!"
2. **Urging [*'araḍ*].** *Example:* "Why not stay with us?"
3. **Oaths [*qasam*].** *Example:* "By God, I *will* do such-and-such!"

Clarifying Literal and Figurative

(فصل) (ومن وجه آخر ينقسمُ إلى: حقيقة ومجاز).

(فالحقيقةُ: ما بَقِيَ في الاستعمال على موضوعه. وقيل: ما استعمل فيما اصطُلح عليه من المخاطبة) وإن لم يبق على موضوعه كالصلاة في الهيئة المخصوصة، فإنه لم يبق على موضوعه اللغوي، وهو الدعاء بخير، والدابة لذات الأربع كالحمار، فإنه لم يبق على موضوعه، وهو كل ما يدب على الأرض.

(والمجازُ: ما تُجُوِّزَ به عن موضوعه) هذا على المعنى الأول للحقيقة وعلى الثاني هو ما استعمل في غير ما اصطلح عليه من المخاطبة.

From another perspective, phrases divide into:

1. **literal; and**
2. **figurative.**

Literal [*al-haqīqah*] is that whose usage remains according to its original meaning [*mawḍū'*]; or [a second definition]: that which is used according to the convention of its audience even if it did not remain upon its original meaning. *Examples: al-ṣalāt* as the specific form [of motions and sayings], since it did not remain upon its original linguistic meaning which is "supplicating for goodness"; and *al-dābah*, for quadrupeds (including donkeys), since it did not remain upon its original meaning of everything walking the earth.

Figurative [*al-majāz*] is that which has exceeded – that which has extended – **its conventional meaning.** This is based on the first meaning of "literal." Based on the second [meaning], it is that which is used in other than what its audience agreed upon.

(والحقيقةُ: إمّا لغويّةٌ) بأن وضعها أهل اللغة كالأسد للحيوان المفترس، (وإما شرعيّةٌ) بأن وضعها الشارع كالصلاة للعبادة المخصوصة، (وإما عرفيّةٌ) بأن وضعها أهل العرف العام كالدابة لذات الأربع كالحمار، وهي لغة لكل ما يدب على الأرض. أو الخاص كالفاعل للاسم المرفوع عند النحاة. وهذا التقسيم ماشٍ على التعريف الثاني للحقيقة دون الأول القاصر على اللغوية.

Literal phrases are either:

1. **Linguistic** – in that it was established by speakers of the language. *Example:* "lion" for the predatory animal.
2. **Legal** – in that it was established by the Legislator (God or the Prophet (May Allah bless him and give him peace)). *Example: al-ṣalāt* for the particular act of worship (trans.: instead of its original meaning which include supplication).
3. **Conventional** – in that it was established by:
    1. General convention. *Example:* the word *dābah* for quadrupeds (like donkeys) while linguistically it is everything walking the earth.
    2. Particular convention. *Example:* grammarians using "subject" for a particular type of noun.

Dividing it in this way works according to the second definition for "literal," but not the first definition which is limited to the linguistic.

(والمجاز إمّا أنْ يكونَ بزيادة، أو نقصان، أو نقل، أو استعارة.)

(فالمجازُ بالزِّيادة مثلُ قوله تعالى: ﴿لَيْسَ كَمِثْلِهِ شَيْءٌ﴾) فالكاف زائدة وإلا فهي بمعنى مثل فيكون له تعالى مثل وهو محال، والقصد بهذا الكلام نفيه.

(والمجازُ بالنّقصان مثلُ قوله تعالى: ﴿وَسْئَلِ الْقَرْيَةَ﴾) أي أهل القرية. وقَرُب صدق تعريف المجاز على ما ذكر بأنه استعمل نفي مثل المثل في نفي المثل وسؤال القرية في سؤال أهلها.

(والمجازُ بالنّقل: كـ«الْغَائِطِ» فيما يخرج من الإنسان) نقل إليه عن حقيقته وهي المكان المطمئن [من الأرض] تقضى فيه الحاجة بحيث لا يتبادر منه عرفاً إلا الخارج.

(والمجازُ بالاستعارة كقوله تعالى: ﴿جِدَارًا يُرِيدُ أَنْ يَنقَضَّ﴾) أي يسقط فشبه ميله إلى السقوط [بإرادة السقوط] التي هي من صفات الحي دون الجماد. والمجاز المبني على التشبيه يسمى استعارة.

Figurative is by means of either:

1. **Addition [*ziyādah*].**
2. **Deletion [*naqṣān*].**
3. **Transfer [*naql*].**
4. **Borrowing [*isti'ārah*].**

***Figurative by addition* is like the Quranic verse, *Nothing like* [kāf] *what is identical* [mithl] *unto Him* (Quran, 42:11).** Here "like" [*kāf*] is [grammatically] superfluous, otherwise it means "similar" [*mithl*]. So there would be something identical to God (which is impossible!) while the point of the phrase is to deny this.

***Figurative by deletion* is like the Quranic verse, *Ask the village* (Quran, 12:82)** – meaning "the people of the village".

These [two verses] evince the correctness of defining metaphor as it was above, since negating something identical to what is identical was used to negate something identical, and asking the village was used for asking its people.

***Figurative by transfer* is like using the word *ghā'iṭ* for feces.** Here it was transferred away from its literal meaning – a depressed spot wherein a person relieves himself – such that by convention, nothing comes to mind other than feces.

***Figurative by borrowing* is like the Quranic verse, *...A wall wanting to collapse* (Quran, 18:77)** (i.e., topple over). Here "being on the verge of toppling" is likened to "it wanting to collapse" which is a characteristic of the living, not the inanimate. So here, the cause for the wall's collapsing has been borrowed and attributed to the wall. Metaphor built upon resemblance is called "borrowing" [*isti'ārah*].

3

COMMANDS

الأوامر والنواهي

(باب) (والأمرُ استدعاءُ الفعل بالقول ممّن هو دونه، على سبيل الوجوب.) فإن كان الاستدعاء من المساوي سمي التماساً أو من الأعلى سمي سؤالاً ، وإن لم يكن على سبيل الوجوب بأن جوز الترك فظاهره أنه ليس بأمر أي في الحقيقة.

A command is using an utterance to demand an action from someone who is inferior, in a way that conveys obligation. When a command is directed to an equal, it is a request [*iltimās*]; when directed to a superior it is a plea [*su'āl*]. When the imperative is not phrased in a way that conveys obligation – in that it is permissible to omit it – the most apparent opinion is that it is not an imperative in the literal sense.

(والصّيغةُ الدّالةُ عليه «افْعَلْ») نحو اضرب وأكرم واشرب.

The verbal form for conveying commands is *if'al* (trans.: the verbal imperative, which is language dependent.) *Examples: iḍrib!, akrim!,* and *ishrab!* ["strike!," "honor!," and "drink!"].

(وهي عند الإطلاق والتّجرّد عن القرينة تحمل عليه)، أي على الوجوب نحو: ﴿وَأَقِيمُوا الصَّلَاةَ﴾ (إلاّ ما دلّ الدّليلُ على أنّ المرادَ منه النّدبُ أو الإباحةُ، فيحمل عليه) أي على الندب أو الإباحة. مثال الندب ﴿فَكَاتِبُوهُمْ إِنْ عَلِمْتُمْ

فِيهِمْ خَيْرًا﴾، ومثال الإباحة ﴿وَإِذَا حَلَلْتُمْ فَاصْطَادُوا﴾ ، وقد أجمعوا على عدم وجوب الكتابة والاصطياد.

When a command is categorical and free of contextual circumstances that obviate it from being a demand for the action, **it is interpreted to convey obligation** (*Example: Establish the prayer* (Quran, 17:78)) **unless there is evidence indicating that what is intended is its recommendedness or its permissibility. [If there is such evidence,] that is how it is interpreted.** That is: as commended or permissibility. An *example* of it being recommended is the Quranic verse, *Conclude a contract with them to set them free if you know they are good* (Quran, 24:33). An *example* of permissibility is, *When you leave the state of pilgrim consecration, then hunt* (Quran, 5:2) – since there is consensus it is not obligatory to agree to set free a slave, or to hunt.

(ولا يقتضي التّكرارَ على الصّحيح)، لأن ما قصد به من تحصيل المأمور به يتحقق بالمرة الواحدة، والأصل براءة الذمة مما زاد عليها، (إلاّ إذا دلّ الدّليلُ على قَصْدِ التّكرار) فيعمل به كالأمر بالصلوات الخمس، والأمر بصوم رمضان.

ومقابل الصحيح أنه يقتضي التكرار، فيستوعب المأمور بالمطلوب ما يمكنه من زمان العمر، حيث لا بيان لأمد المأمور به، لانتفاء مرجح بعضه على بعض.

A command does not entail repetition, according to the sound position, because the objective – that what has been commanded occur – occurs through a single time, and the default is that one is not responsible for anything exceeding a single time, **unless there is evidence indicating that repetition is intended** in which case it is acted upon, e.g., the order to pray the five prayers and to fast Ramaḍān.

The opposite to the sound position is that commands entail repetition. So, the person ordered spends all possible time performing the required action as long as there is no clarification for the extent of what has been ordered. This is from there being nothing that makes [its performance in] one time preponderant over other times.

(ولا يقتضي الفَوْر)، [لأن الغرض منه إيجاد الفعل من غير اختصاص بالزمان الأول دون الزمان الثاني]. وقيل يقتضي الفور، وعلى ذلك بني قول من قال يقتضي التكرار.

Commands do not entail immediacy, since the goal is the action's existence without it being specific to the first time and not the next. There is an opinion that it entails immediacy. Those who hold that it entails repetition say that it entails immediacy.

(والأمرُ بإيجاد الفعل أمرٌ به، وبما لا يتمُّ الفعلُ إلاّ به، كالأمر بالصّلوات أمرٌ بالطّهارة المؤدّيةِ إليها) فإن الصلاة لا تصح بدون الطهارة.

The command to bring about the existence of the action is a command to perform it and everything which it requires in order to be carried out. For example, the command to perform prayer is a command to perform the purification which leads to it, since prayer is not valid without it.

(وإذا فُعِلَ) بالبناء للمفعول، أي المأمور به (يخرج المأمورُ عن العهدة) ويتصف الفعل بالإجزاء.

If the command is performed (i.e., the ordered action), **the [person] ordered is cleared of the injunction** – from the order's injunction, and the performance is described as sufficient.

Who Commands and Prohibitions Include

(باب) الذي يدخل في الأمر والنهي [وما لا يدخل] هذه ترجمة. (ويدخلُ في خطاب الله تعالى المؤمنون) وسيأتي الكلام في الكفار.

(والسّاهي، والصّبي، والمجنونُ غيرُ داخلين في الخطاب) لانتفاء التكليف عنهم. ويؤمر الساهي بعد ذهاب السهو عنه بجبر خلل السهو، كقضاء ما فاته من الصلاة، وضمان ما أتلفه من المال.

Believers enter [within the scope of] the speech of God (Mighty and Majestic is He!). The subject of disbelievers will come.

Those who are forgetful, minors, or insane (Ibn Qāsim: or unconscious) **do not enter into those addressed** since legal responsibility has been lifted from them. Once someone ceases to be forgetful [for example], he is ordered to rectify what was missed during his forgetfulness, like making up missed prayers and reimbursing damaged property.

(والكفّارُ مخاطبون بفروع الشّريعة، وبما لا تصحّ إلاّ به، وهو الإسلامُ، لقوله تعالى) [حكاية عن الكفار]: ﴿مَا سَلَكَكُمْ فِي سَقَرَ، قَالُوا لَمْ نَكُ مِنَ الْمُصَلِّيْنَ﴾) وفائدة خطابهم بها عقابهم عليها إذ لا تصح منهم حال الكفر لتوقفها على النية المتوقفة على الإسلام ولا يؤاخذون بها بعد الإسلام ترغيباً فيه.

Non-believers are intended recipients of the particulars of Sacred Law and of that which is required for its valid performance – Islam – because of the Quranic verse, "*What led you into the flame?*" *They will say:* "*Because we were not of those who prayed...*" (Quran, 74:42–3). (trans.: The verses continue: "*Nor were we of whose who fed the poor, But we used to talk of vanities with vain talkers, And we used to deny the Day of Requital, Till certainty [death] overtook us*" (Quran, 74:44–47).)

The significance of them being addressed by this verse is their punishment for these actions, since it is not valid for them to perform them because the actions are dependent upon intention, which is dependent upon Islam. These actions are not held against them after entering Islam as an enticement to enter Islam.

(والأمرُ بالشّيء نَهْيٌ عن ضدِّه، والنّهْيُ عن الشيء أمرٌ بضدّه). فإذا قال له: اسكن كان ناهياً له عن التحرك، أو لا تتحرك، كان آمراً له بالسكون.

The command to perform something specific is a prohibition from performing its opposite. The prohibition of performing something specific is a command to perform its opposite. So, if he is told, "Remain still!" it is a prohibition from moving. And if he is told, "Don't move!" it is a command to remain motionless. (trans.: This is when there is only one alternative. When there are several alternatives, then it is known with certainty that one of them gets the opposite ruling, but it is unsure which one.)

Prohibitions

(باب) (والنّهْيُ استدعاءٌ. أي: طلب التَّرْكِ بالقول ممّن هو دونه، على سبيل الوجوب)، على وزان ما تقدم في حد الأمر.

ويدل النهي المطلق شرعاً على فساد المنهي عنه في العبادات، سواء نهي عنها لعينها [كصلاة الحائض وصومها أو لأمر لازم لها كصوم يوم النحر والصلاة في الأوقات المكروهة. وفي المعاملات إن رجع إلى نفس العقد كما في بيع الحصاة. أو لأمر داخل فيه كبيع الملاقيح أو لأمر خارج عنه لازم له كما في بيع درهم بدرهمين، فإن كان غير لازم له، كالوضوء بالماء المغصوب مثلاً، وكالبيع وقت نداء الجمعة لم يدل على الفساد خلافاً لما يفهمه كلام المصنف]

A prohibition is using an utterance to invite (i.e., request) an action from an inferior, in a way that conveys obligation. It follows what preceded concerning the definition of commands.

Categorical prohibitions indicate – in the legal sense – the invalidity of the prohibited thing with respect to acts of worship – whether it itself was prohibited (e.g., a woman praying or fasting during menses), or because of something it entails (e.g., fasting on the Day of Immolation [*Yaum al-Naḥr*], and praying during the times wherein it is offensive to do so).

With respect to transactions, [prohibition indicates invalidity] if it goes back to the contract itself, (e.g., buying whatever a tossed pebble happens to fall on), or because of something intrinsic (e.g., selling an animal which has not yet been born), or because of something external to which it is inextricably linked (e.g., such as selling one Dirham for two).

But if the prohibited matter is not inextricably linked (e.g., making ablution with stolen water, and buying during the time of Friday Prayer), it does not indicate invalidity – contrary to what the author's phrasing indicates.

(وتردُ صيغةُ الأمر، والمرادُ به الإباحة) كما تقدمَ، (أو التّهديدُ) نحو ﴿اعْمَلُوا مَا شِئْتُمْ﴾، (أو التّسويةُ) نحو ﴿فَاصْبِرُوا أَوْ لَا تَصْبِرُوا﴾، (أو التّكوينُ) نحو ﴿كُونُوا قِرَدَةً﴾.

The verbal phrase for commands may be mentioned (i.e., occur) **while what is intended** by the imperative **is:**

- **Mere permissibility.** (As preceded.)
- **A threat.** *Example: Do as you will,* (Quran, 41:40).
- **Equality between two things.** *Example: Be patient or impatient,* (Quran, 52:16).
- **Spontaneous formation.** *Example: Be ye apes!,* (Quran, 2:65).

4

UNIVERSAL AND PARTICULAR APPLICABILITY

العام والخاص

(باب) (وأمّا العامّ فهو ما عمّ شيئَيْنِ فصاعدًا) من غير حصر ، (من قوله: «عممْتُ زيدًا وعَمْرًا بالعطاء»، و«عممْتُ جميعَ النّاس بالعطاء») أي شملتهم به، ففي العام شمول.

Universal applicability [*'āmm*] is what includes two or more things without constraint. **[It comes] from the phrase "I included Zayd and Omar with the gift," and "I included men in their entirety with the gift"** (that is: "I included them with it"), since universality includes comprehensiveness.

(وألفاظه) الموضوعة له (أربعة:)

(الاسمُ المعرَّفُ بالألف واللّام) ، نحو ﴿إِنَّ الْإِنْسَانَ لَفِي خُسْرٍ إِلَّا الَّذِينَ ءَامَنُوا﴾ .

(واسمُ الجمعِ المعرَّفُ باللّام) نحو ﴿وَقَاتِلُوا الْمُشْرِكِينَ﴾ .

(والأسماءُ المبهمةُ كـ«مَنْ» فيمن يَعْقِلُ و«مَا» فيما لا يعقلُ) كمن دخل داري فهو آمن، (و«وأيّ» في الجميع) أي من يعقل وما لا عقل، نحو أي عبيدي جاءك أحسن إليه، وأي الأشياء أردت أعطيتكه، (و«أَيْنَ» في المكان) نحو أين ما تكن أكن معك، (و«مَتَى» في الزمان) نحو متى شئت جئتك، (و«مَا» في الاستفهام)

نحو ما عندك؟ (والجزاء) نحو ما تعمل تجز به، وفي نسخة والخبر بدل الجزاء نحو علمت ما عملت، (وغيره) كالخبر على النسخة الأولى والجزاء على الثانية.

(و«لاَ» في النّكرات) النكرات نحو لا رجل في الدار.

The phrases established for universal applicability **are four:**

1. Singular **nouns made definite using the definite article [*alif-lām*].** *Example:* Man [*al-insān*] *is indeed in loss, except those who believe and do good works,* (Quran, 103:2–3).
2. **Mass nouns made definite by the definite article.** *Example: Fight the* polytheists, (Quran, 9:36).
3. **Ambiguous nouns, like:**
    1. **"Whoever" for sentient beings.** *Example:* "Whoever enters my house is safe."
    2. **"whatever" for non-sentient beings.** *Example:* "Whatever came to me from you, I have taken it."
    3. **"whichever" interrogative, conditional, or appositive for them both** (i.e., sentient and non-sentient). *Examples:* "Whichever of my slaves comes to you, be good to him," and, "Whichever you desire, I give it to you."
    4. **"wherever" for the spatial.** *Example:* "Wherever you are, I am with you."
    5. **"whenever" for the temporal.** *Example:* "Whenever you wish, I will come to you."
    6. **"whatever" for interrogatives** *Example:* "Whatever do you have?"
    7. **"whatever" with consequences** *Example:* "Whatever you do, you will be rewarded for." Another version of the manuscript has the word "predicates" instead of "consequences," [and based on that the commentary is:] (e.g., "I will do whatever you do"); **and**
    8. **Other things** – such as "predicates" following the first version of the manuscript, and "rewards" following the second version.
4. **The negative with indefinite nouns.** *Example:* "No man is in the house."

(والعموم من صفات النُّطق، ولا يجوز دعوى العموم في غيره من الفعل وما يجري مجراه) كما في جمعه ﷺ بين الصلاتين في السفر رواه البخاري، فإنه لا يعم السفر الطويل والقصير، فإنه إنما يقع في واحد منهما. وكما في قضائه ﷺ بالشفعة للجار. رواه النسائي عن الحسن مرسلاً، فإنه لا يعم كل جار، لاحتمال خصوصية في ذلك الجار.

(والخاصُّ يقابلُ العامَّ) فيقال فيه ما لا يتناول شيئين فصاعداً من غير حصر، نحو رجل ورجلين وثلاثة رجال.

Universal applicability is an attribute of utterances. It is not permissible to claim universal applicability for actions and other things which take their course. *Examples:* [1] The Prophet (May Allah bless him and give him peace) combined between two prayers while traveling which is in Bukhārī.[1] [It cannot be a case of universal applicability] since the action does not include both long and short journeys since it took place in only one of the two. [2] The Prophet (May Allah bless him and give him peace) ruled that the neighbor is entitled to pre-emption of a sale [*shuf'ah*] which was narrated by Nasā'ī via Ḥasan in an expedient report [*mursal*],[2] since it does not include every neighbor due to the possibility of something particular to that [particular] neighbor.

Particular applicability [*al-khāṣṣ*] is the opposite of universal applicability. So it is said: that which does not include two or more things without constraint. *Examples:* "one man," "two men," and "three men."

Particular Applicability

(باب) (والتّخصيصُ تمييزُ بعضِ الجملة) أي إخراجه كإخراج المعاهدين من قوله تعالى: ﴿فَاقْتُلُوا الْمُشْرِكِينَ﴾.

---

1 Bukhārī (1107–8).

2 I could not locate this specific report in Nasī'ī, however similar reports are narrated in Aḥmed (3/303), Abū Dāwūd (3517–8), Tirmidhī (1368–9), Ibn Mājah (2493), Ibn Ḥibbān (7/309), Nasā'ī (7/301).

(وهو ينقسمُ إلى مّتصل، ومنفصل).

(فالمتّصلُ: الاستثناءُ) وسيأتي مثاله، (والشّرطُ) نحو أكرم بني تميم إن جاؤوك، أي الجائين منهم، (والتّقييدُ بالصّفة) نحو أكرم بني تميم الفقهاء.

Particularization [*takhṣīṣ*] is distinguishing part of the sentence (i.e., removing it). *Example:* removing those who had a pact from His statement, *Fight the polytheists,* (Quran, 9:5).[3]

[Phrases for] declaring something particular are divided into connected (trans.: dependent clauses which, syntactically, cannot stand on its own and are, rather, subordinate to phrases containing universal applicability), **and disjointed** (trans.: independent clauses which, syntactically, can stand on their own and are not subordinate to the phrases containing universal applicability which they modify).

Connected particularization includes:

1. **Exceptions.** (Its example will come.);
2. **Conditionals.** *Example:* "Honor Banī Tamīm if they come to you," i.e., "[honor] those of them who come."
3. **Qualification using an attribute.** *Example:* "Honor the legists of Banī Tamīm."

(والاستثناءُ إخراجُ ما لولاه لدخل في الكلام) نحو جاء القوم إلا زيداً. (وإنما يصحُّ الاستثناءُ بشرط أنْ يبقى من المستثنى منه شيءٌ) نحو له عليَّ عشرة إلا تسعة، فلو قال إلا عشرة، لم يصح، وتلزمه العشرة.

(ومن شرطه أنْ يكونَ متصلاً بالكلام) فلو قال جاء الفقهاء، ثم قال بعد يوم إلا زيداً، لم يصح.

---

3 The particularization occurs in the first verse of the chapter: [*This is a declaration of*] *disassociation, from God and His Messenger, to those with whom you had made a treaty among the polytheists,* (Quran, 9:1).

(ويجوزُ تقديمُ المستثنى على المستثنى منه) نحو ما قام إلا زيداً أحدٌ.

(ويجوز الاستثناءُ من الجنس، كما تقدّم، ومن غيره) نحو جاء القوم إلا الحمير.

(والشّرط) المخصص (يجوزُ أن يتقدّم على المشروط) نحو إن جاءك بنو تميم فأكرمهم.

Excepting [*istithnā'*] is removing something that otherwise would have been included by the phrase. *Example:* "The group came, except Zayd."

Excepting is valid only with the condition that something remains from *that which the exclusion is being made.* *Example:* "I owe him ten *dinars* except nine". If he were to say, "...excluding ten" it would be invalid and he would owe ten.

One of its conditions is that it be linked to the phrase. So it would not be valid if one were to say, "The legists came," and one day later said, "except Zayd."

It is permissible to put *that which is excluded before that from which it is excluded.* *Example:* "Except Zayd, no one stood."

It is permissible to exclude from the [same] category [*jins*] - as was mentioned above - and from other things. *Example:* "The people came, excluding the donkeys."

Conditionals that have exclusions **are permitted to precede that which is stipulated by it.** *Example:* "If Banī Tamīm come to you, honor them."

(والمقيّدُ بالصّفة يُحملُ عليه المطلق، كـ«الرَّقَبَة» قُيِّدَتْ بالإيمان في بعض المواضع) كما في كفارة القتل، وأطلقت في بعض المواضع، [كما في كفارة الظهار] (فيُحملُ المطلقُ على المقيّد) احتياطاً.

[When] something is qualified by an attribute, the unqualified is interpreted as [being similarly] qualified, such as a slave qualified by "belief" in some places (*example:* concerning expiation for murder[4]); and unqualified in others (*example:* concerning the expiation for likening one's wife to his mother [*al-ẓihār*][5]) – **thus the unqualified is interpreted as agreeing with the qualified** as a precautionary measure.

What Can Be Rendered Particular and By What

(باب) (ويجوز تخصيصُ الكتاب بالكتاب) نحو قوله تعالى: ﴿وَلَا تَنْكِحُوا الْمُشْرِكَاتِ﴾، خصَّ بقوله تعالى: ﴿وَالْمُحْصَنَاتُ مِنَ الَّذِينَ أُوتُوا الْكِتَابَ مِنْ قَبْلِكُمْ﴾ أي حلٌّ لكم، (وتخصيصُ الكتاب بالسّنّة) كتخصيص قوله تعالى: ﴿يُوصِيكُمُ اللهُ فِي أَوْلَادِكُم﴾ إلى آخر الآية الشامل للولد الكافر بحديث الصحيحين: «لا يرث المسلم الكافر ولا الكافر المسلم»، (وتخصيصُ السّنّة بالكتاب) [كتخصيص حديث الصحيحين: «لا يقبل الله صلاة أحدكم إذا أحدث حتى يتوضأ»، بقوله تعالى: ﴿وَإِنْ كُنْتُمْ مَرْضَى﴾ إلى قوله ﴿فَلَمْ تَجِدُوا مَاءً فَتَيَمَّمُوا﴾ وإن وردت السنة بالتيمم أيضاً بعد نزول الآية]، (وتخصيص السّنّة بالسّنّة) كتخصيص حديث الصحيحين: «فيما سقت السماء العشر» بحديثهما «ليس فيما دون خمسة أوسق صدقة»، (وتخصيصُ النّطْقِ بالقياس).

(ونعني بالنّطق قولَ الله تعالى، وقول الرّسول ﷺ) لأن القياس يستند إلى نص من كتاب أو سنة فكأنه المخصص.

It is possible for:

1. **The Quran to be rendered particular by the Quran.** *Example: Do not marry idolatrous women,* (Quran, 2:221) which is

---

4 ...*the freeing of* a believing slave and a compensation payment presented to the deceased's family... (Quran, 4:92).

5 ...*the freeing of* a slave before they touch one another. (Quran, 58:3).

restricted by *And the virtuous women of those who received the Book before you,* (Quran, 5:5), i.e., are lawful for you.

2. **The Quran to be rendered particular by the *sunna*.** *Example: God thus commands you concerning [the division] for your children* (Quran, 4:11) until the end of the verse – which is inclusive of the children of the disbelievers – being excluded by the hadith in Bukhārī and Muslim, "Muslims do not pass inheritance to non-Muslims, nor non-Muslims to Muslims."[6]
3. **The *sunna* to be rendered particular by the Quran.** *Example:* the hadith: "God does not accept prayer from any of you when they lose ritual purity until they make ablution,"[7] being excluded by *And if ye be ill ... and you find not water, then take clean earth* (Quran, 4:43) – even if the *sunna* also mentioned dry ablution after the verse was revealed.
4. **The *sunna* to be rendered particular by the *sunna*.** *Example:* the hadith: "[A *zakāt* of] one tenth from anything irrigated by the sky,"[8] being excluded by the hadith "There is no *ṣadaqah* in anything less than five *awsaq*."[9]
5. **Utterances to be rendered particular by analogical reasoning. By "utterances" we mean the words of God (Mighty and Majestic is He!) and of the Messenger (May Allah bless him and give him peace).** This argument is that analogical reasoning rests upon a text from the Book of God or a Sunna, so it is as though the text [performs] the exclusion.

---

6 Bukhārī (6764), Muslim (1614).
7 Bukhārī (6954), Muslim (225).
8 Bukhārī (1483), Muslim (981).
9 Bukhārī (1484), Muslim (979).

5

AMBIGUITY & CLARIFICATION

المجمل والمبين، والظاهر والمؤول

(باب) (والمُجْمَلُ: ما يفتقرُ إلى البيان) نحو ﴿ ثَلَاثَةَ قُرُوءٍ﴾ فإنه يحتمل الأطهار والحيض لاشتراك القرء بين الحيض والطهر.

(والبيانُ: إخراجُ الشّيء من حيّز الإشكال إلى حيّز التّجلّي) الاتضاح [والمبين هو النص].

Ambiguity [*mujmal*] is that which is in need of clarification. *Example:* "three periods [*qurū'*]," since it is possible to interpret "period" as "purity from menstruation" or "menstruation," since [the word] *qur'* shares the meaning of menstruation and purity [from menstruation].

Clarification [*al-bayān*] is taking something from the realm of ambiguity into the realm of being evident (i.e., clarification).

Something clear [*mubayyin*] is called unequivocal [*naṣṣ*].

(والنّصُّ: ما لا يحتملُ إلاّ معنىً واحدًا) كزيد في رأيت زيداً، (وقيل: ما تأويلُه تنزيلُه) نحو ﴿فَصِيَامُ ثَلَاثَةِ أَيَّامٍ﴾ ، فإنه بمجرد ما ينزل يفهم معناه.

(وهو مشتق من «مِنصّة العروس»، وهو الكرسيُّ) لارتفاعه على غيره في فهم معناه من غير توقف.

The unequivocal [*naṣṣ*] is that which cannot be interpreted except as having one single meaning (*example:* "Zayd" in "I saw Zayd"); **or: whose interpretation is [just] as it was revealed.** *Example:* "Fasting three days," since its meaning is understood just by it being revealed.

[The Arabic technical term *naṣṣ*] is derived from *minaṣṣat al-ʿurūs*, which is the platform because it towers above everything else when it comes to understanding its meaning without [considerable] thought.

Evident & Interpreted

(والظّاهرُ ما احتمل أمرَين، أحدُهما أظهرُ من الآخر) كالأسد في رأيت اليوم أسداً، فإنه ظاهر في الحيوان المفترس، لأن المعنى الحقيقي محتمل للرجل الشجاع بدله.

فإن حمل اللفظ على المعنى الآخر سمي مؤولاً وإنما يؤول بالدليل كما قال.

(ويؤوّلُ الظّاهرُ بالدّليل، ويسمّى ظاهرًا بالدّليل) أي كما يسمى مؤولاً، ومنه قوله تعالى: ﴿وَالسَّمَاءَ بَنَيْنَاهَا بِأَيْيدٍ﴾ ظاهره جمع يد، وذلك محال في حق الله تعالى فصرف إلى معنى القوة بالدليل العقلي القاطع.

Evident [*al-ẓāhir*] is that which can be interpreted in two ways, where one [interpretation] is more preponderant than the other. *Example:* "lion" in the phrase, "Today I saw a lion," since it is probably the predatory animal as this is the literal meaning, and interpretable as "the brave man" instead.

When the phrase is interpreted as the other meaning, it is called "interpreted" [*ta'wīl*]. It is only done with the use of evidence, just as the author said:

Evident [*ẓāhir*] is interpreted if there is evidence. It is called "evident through evidence" [*ẓāhiran bi-l-dalīl*]. It is also called "interpreted" [*mu'awwal*]. It includes *And the sky: We built the heaven with our hands* (Quran, 51:47). Its apparent meaning is the plural of "hand" [*yad*], but this is impossible with respect to God (Mighty and Majestic is He!), so it is diverted to mean "might [*quwwa*]" via clear, sure [*qaṭʿī*] rational evidence.

6

ACTIONS OF THE PROPHET ﷺ

الأفعال

(باب) لأفعال هذه ترجمة

(فعل صاحبِ الشّريعة) يعني النبي ﷺ (لا يخلو:)

(إمّا أَنْ يكونَ على وجه القُرْبَةِ والطّاعة) [أو لا يكون].

[فإن كان على وجه القربة والطاعة]، (فإن دلّ الدّليل على الاختصاص به يحمل على الاختصاص) كزيادته ﷺ في النكاح على أربع نسوة، (وإن لم يدلّ دليلٌ لا يخصّص به، لأن الله تعالى قال: ﴿لَقَدْ كَانَ لَكُمْ فِي رَسُولِ اللَّهِ أُسْوَةٌ حَسَنَةٌ﴾، فيُحمل على الوجوب عند بعض أصحابنا) في حقه وحقنا لأنه الأحوط، (ومِنْهم مَنْ قال: يحمل على الندب) لأنه المتحقق بعد الطلب، (ومِنْهم مَنْ قال: يُتَوَقَفُ فيه) لتعارض الأدلة في ذلك.

(فإن كان على وجهٍ غيرِ وجهِ القربةِ والطّاعة فيُحمَل على الإباحة) في حقه وحقنا.

The actions of the Legislator (the Prophet ﷺ) **are either in the manner of acts of worship and obedience, or not.**

If they are in the manner of acts of worship and obedience and there is evidence indicating it being particular to him ﷺ, then it is interpreted as being particular [to him ﷺ]. For example, his marrying more than four women ﷺ.

If no evidence indicates this [that it is particular to him ﷺ], then the action is not particular to him ﷺ, because of the Quranic verse,

In the messenger of God you have a good example for him who hopes in God and the Last Day, and remembers God much.[1] **[The action] is interpreted as being obligatory according to some of our [Shāfi'ī] colleagues** with respect to him ﷺ and us, since it is the most precautionary. Some of our colleagues say that the action is interpreted as being recommended, since this is what is clear after the established request. (trans.: The verse cited at the beginning supports the view of it being recommended, according to al-Juwaynī in his own commentary on the work.) **Some of our colleagues opined that one must withhold judgment** since the relevant evidence is inconsistent.

If the action is not in the manner of worship and obedience, then it is interpreted as being merely permissible (e.g., eating and drinking) – with respect to him ﷺ and us.

(وإقرارُ صاحبِ الشّريعة ﷺ على القول) من أحد (هو [كـ]قول صاحبِ الشّريعة ﷺ، وإقرارُه على الفعل كفعله) لأنه معصوم عن أن يقر أحداً على منكر، مثال ذلك إقراره ﷺ أبا بكر على قوله بإعطاء سلب القتيل لقاتله، وإقراره خالد بن الوليد على أكل الضب متفق عليهما.

The tacit approval [*iqrār*] of the Legislator ﷺ of a statement from any individual **is the statement of the Legislator** ﷺ (i.e., just like his statement), **and his endorsement of an action** from any individual **is just as his [own] action.** This is because the Prophet ﷺ is divinely protected from tacitly approving someone doing something objectionable. *Examples:* his tacit approval of Abū Bakr (May Allah be pleased with him) giving the belongings of a slain enemy combatant to his slayer,[2] and his approving of Khālid ibn al-Walīd eating desert iguana [*ḍabb*] – which is in both Bukhārī and Muslim.[3]

---

1 Quran, 33:21.
2 Bukhārī (4192, 4321), Muslim (1751).
3 Bukhārī (5400, 5537), Muslim (1945).

(وما فُعل في وقته ﷺ، في غير مجلسه، وعلم به، ولم ينكرْهُ، فحكمُهُ كحكم ما فُعِلَ في مجلسه) كعلمه بحلف أبي بكر - رضي الله عنه - أنه لا يأكل الطعام في وقت غيظه ثم أكل لما رأى الأكل خيراً، كما يؤخذ من حديث مسلم في الأطعمة.

The ruling of things done while he (May Allah bless him and give him peace) was alive yet not in his presence, and that he ﷺ knew of yet did not reject, is the same as something done in his presence [*majlis*]. *Example:* that he ﷺ knew that Abū Bakr (May Allah be pleased with him) swore an oath that he would not eat food for the duration of his anger, and Abū Bakr then eating when he realized that eating was better for him, just as is understood from the hadith concerning feeding.[4]

4 Muslim (2057).

7

ABROGATION

النسخ

(باب) (وأمّا النّسخُ فمعناه الإزالةُ. يقال: «نَسَخَتِ الشَّمْسُ الظِّلَّ» إذا أزالَتْهُ. وقيل: معناه النقل من قولهم: «نَسَخْتُ مَا فِي هَذَا الْكِتَابِ» إذا نقلتُهُ بأشكال كتابته).

The linguistic **meaning of abrogation [*naskh*] is "to efface." One says, "the sun effaced the shadow" when it removes it** and erases it by its rising. **It is also said that it comes from "to transfer," from the saying, "I transferred what was in the book" when he transfers it in the manner in which it was written.**

(وحدُّهُ: الخطابُ الدّالُّ على رفع الحكم الثّابت بالخطاب المتقدِّم على وجه لولاه لكان ثابتًا مع تراخيه عنه) ويؤخذ منه حد النسخ بأنه رفع الحكم المذكور بخطاب إلى آخره، أي رفع تعلقه بالفعل، فخرج بقوله الثابت بالخطاب، رفع الحكم الثابت بالبراءة الأصلية، أي عدم التكليف بشيء.

وبقولنا بخطاب المأخوذ من كلامه الرفع بالموت والجنون.

وبقوله على وجه إلى آخره، ما لو كان الخطاب الأول مغياً بغاية أو معللاً بمعنى، وصرح الخطاب الثاني بمقتضى ذلك .

فإنه لا يسمى ناسخاً [للأول مثاله] قوله تعالى: ﴿إِذَا نُودِيَ لِلصَّلَاةِ مِنْ يَوْمِ الْجُمُعَةِ فَاسْعَوْا إِلَى ذِكْرِ اللَّهِ وَذَرُوا الْبَيْعَ﴾ ، فتحريم البيع مغيا بانقضاء الجمعة، فلا يقال إن قوله تعالى: ﴿فَإِذَا قُضِيَتِ الصَّلَاةُ فَانْتَشِرُوا فِي الْأَرْضِ وَابْتَغُوا مِنْ فَضْلِ اللَّهِ﴾ ناسخ للأول بل بيّن غاية التحريم.

وكذا قوله تعالى: ﴿وَحُرِّمَ عَلَيْكُمْ صَيْدُ الْبَرِّ ما دُمْتُمْ حُرُمًا﴾ لا يقال نسخه قوله تعالى: ﴿وَإِذَا حَلَلْتُمْ فَاصْطَادُوا﴾ لأن التحريم للإحرام وقد زال.

وخرج بقوله مع تراخيه عنه، ما اتصل بالخطاب من صفة أو شرط أو استثناء.

Its legal **definition is a discourse [*khiṭāb*] indicating the subsequent repeal of a ruling established by a previous discourse, in such a way that without which the ruling would remain established.** This is the definition for "the abrogating." The definition for "abrogation" is taken from it: removing the mentioned ruling through a discourse – that is: removing the ruling's relationship to the actions.

The phrase "established by a discourse," precludes the ruling established by the default ruling of innocence [*barā'at al-aṣliyyah*]: the absence of being responsible for anything [prior to evidence to the contrary].

The phrase "by a discourse" – which is taken from the author's words – precludes the ruling being repealed by death and insanity.

The phrase "in a manner, etc...," precludes a previous discourse that had a set limit or apparent cause [Ar. *'illah*, Latin *ratio legis*] and the second discourse was explicit in entailing that, since this is not named [as] abrogating for the first.

[An *example* for having a set limit] is the Quranic verse, *When the call is heard for the prayer on Friday, hasten to the remembrance of God and cease your trading* (Quran, 62:9). Here the prohibition to sell is limited by completing the performance of the Friday

Prayer, hence it is not said that the verse *And when the prayer is ended, then disperse in the land and seek of God's favor* (Quran, 62:10) abrogates the first. Rather, the second clarifies the limit of the prohibition.

[An *example* for having an apparent cause (*'illah*) is] that the Quranic verse *[Hunting] game is forbidden to you while you are in the state of consecration* [*for pilgrimage*] (Quran, 5:1) is not said to be abrogated by the verse *But when you leave the state of consecration* [*and the sacred precincts around Makkah*], *hunt* [*game*] (Quran, 5:2), since the prohibition is due to Pilgrimage – which has ended.

The phrase "subsequent to it" removes the attributes, conditionals, and exclusions connected to the discourse.

Divisions of Abrogation

(باب) (ويجوزُ نَسْخُ الرّسمِ وبقاءُ الحكم) نحو «الشيخ والشيخة إذا زنيا فارجموهما ألبتة». قال عمر رضي الله عنه: «فإنّا قد قرأناها» رواه الشافعي وغيره. «وقد رجم ﷺ المحصنين» متفق عليه. [وهما المراد بالشيخ والشيخة]، (ونَسْخُ الحكم وبقاء الرّسم) نحو ﴿وَالَّذِينَ يُتَوَفَّوْنَ مِنكُمْ وَيَذَرُونَ أَزْوَاجًا وَصِيَّةً لِأَزْوَاجِهِم مَّتَاعًا إِلَى الْحَوْلِ﴾ نسخ بآية ﴿يَتَرَبَّصْنَ بِأَنفُسِهِنَّ أَرْبَعَةَ أَشْهُرٍ وَعَشْرًا﴾، (ونَسْخُ الأمرين معًا) نحو حديث مسلم عن عائشة رضي الله عنها «كان فيما أنزل عشر رضعات معلومات يحرمن» فنسخن [«بخمس معلومات يحرمن»].

It is possible for:

1. **The written record to be abrogated while its ruling remains.** *Example:* "The married man and married woman: if they commit adultery lapidate them until death." 'Omar (May Allah be pleased with him) said, "Verily, we used to recite it" – al-Shāfi'ī and others narrated it; and "the Messenger of God ﷺ did

lapidate married people" (Bukhārī and Muslim).[1] Married people are what is intended by *"al-shaykh wa al-shaykhah"*.

2. **The ruling to be abrogated while its written record remains.** *Example: Those of your who are about to die and leave behind wives [leave a] bequest to their wives a year's provision, without causing them to leave their homes* (Quran, 2:240), which is abrogated by: *Widows shall wait, keeping themselves apart [before they remarry] for a period of four months and ten days* (Quran, 2:234).
3. **Both [the written record and its ruling] to be abrogated.** *Example:* the hadith narrated from 'Ā'ishah (May God be pleased with her), where she said: "The Revelation included that ten known nursings render [certain relationships] unlawful. This was abrogated by five nursings rendering [the same] unlawful."[2]

Abrogation is divided into that which has a replacement, and that which does not. The first is like facing Jerusalem during prayer being abrogated by facing the Ka'bah. The second will come, like what is in the Quranic verse, *When you consult the Messenger in private, give charity before such consultation* (Quran, 58:12).

(وينقسمُ النّسخُ إلى بدل، وإلى غير بدل) الأول كما في نسخ استقبال بيت المقدس باستقبال الكعبة وسيأتي. والثاني كما في نسخ قوله تعالى: ﴿إِذَا نَاجَيْتُمُ الرَّسُولَ فَقَدِّمُوا بَيْنَ يَدَيْ نَجْوَاكُمْ صَدَقَةً﴾. (وإلى ما هو أغلظ) كنسخ التخيير بين صوم رمضان والفدية إلى تعيين الصوم قال الله تعالى ﴿وَعَلَى الَّذِينَ يُطِيقُونَهُ فِدْيَةٌ﴾ إلى قوله ﴿فَمَنْ شَهِدَ مِنْكُمُ الشَّهْرَ فَلْيَصُمْهُ﴾، (وإلى ما هو أخف) كنسخ قوله تعالى ﴿إِنْ يَكُنْ مِنْكُمْ عِشْرُونَ صَابِرُونَ يَغْلِبُوا مِائَتَيْنِ﴾ بقوله تعالى ﴿فَإِن يَكُن مِّنكُم مِّائَةٌ صَابِرَةٌ يَغْلِبُوا مِائَتَيْنِ﴾.

1 Bukhārī (5271, 6815, 6825, 7167), Muslim (1691).
2 Muslim (1452).

[Abrogation with a replacement is divided into:]

1. **Stricture.** *Example:* choosing between fasting Ramaḍān and paying an expiation being abrogated by fasting being personally obligatory. God (Mighty and Majestic is He!) said: *And for those who can afford it there is a ransom: the feeding of a man in need* (Quran, 2:184) up to: *Therefore whoever of you is present in that month let him fast* (Quran, 2:185).
2. **Leniency.** *Example:* The Quranic verse, *If there be of you twenty steadfast they shall overcome two hundred* (Quran, 8:65) being abrogated by, *if there be of you a steadfast hundred they shall overcome two hundred* (Quran, 8:66). (trans.: These two verses are the verses of steadfastness referred to below.)

(باب) (ويجوزُ نَسْخُ الكتابِ بالكتاب) ما تقدم في آيتي العدة وآيتي المصابرة، (ونسخُ السّنّةِ بالكتاب) كما تقدم في نسخ استقبال بيت المقدس الثابت بالسنة الفعلية كما في حديث الصحيحين بقوله تعالى ﴿فَوَلِّ وَجْهَكَ شَطْرَ الْمَسْجِدِ الْحَرَامِ﴾، (ونسخُ السّنّةِ بالسّنّة) نحو حديث مسلم «كنت نهيتكم عن زيارة القبور فزوروها».

It is possible for:

1. **The Quran to abrogate the Quran.** *Example:* what preceded in the two verses concerning the waiting period,[3] and the two verses of steadfastness.[4]
2. **The Quran to abrogate the Sunna.** *Example:* what preceded concerning facing Jerusalem during prayer which was established via performed Sunna in the hadiths in Bukhārī and Muslim[5] being abrogated by the Quranic verse, *Turn towards the Sacred Mosque* (Quran, 2:144).
3. **The Sunna to abrogate the Sunna.** *Example:* the hadith "I used

3 Quran, 2:240 and 2:234.
4 Quran, 8:65 and 8:66.
5 Bukhārī (399, 4486, 4492, 7252), Muslim (525–7).

to forbid you from visiting graves. Now visit them!"[6]

وسكت عن نسخ الكتاب بالسنة وقد قيل بجوازه ومثل له بقوله تعالى ﴿كُتِبَ عَلَيْكُمْ إِذَا حَضَرَ أَحَدَكُمُ الْمَوْتُ إِنْ تَرَكَ خَيْرًا الْوَصِيَّةُ لِلْوَالِدَيْنِ وَالْأَقْرَبِينَ﴾ مع حديث الترمذي وغيره «لا وصية لوارث». واعترض بأنه خبر واحد، وسيأتي أنه لا ينسخ المتواتر بالآحاد.

وفي نسخة: ولا يجوز نسخ الكتاب بالسنة أي بخلاف تخصيصه بها كما تقدم لأن التخصيص أهون من النسخ.

The author did not mention the Sunna abrogating the Quran. One opinion is that it is possible. An *example* of this was made with [the verse] *It is prescribed for you, when one of you approaches death, if he leaves wealth, that he bequeath it to parents and near relatives* (Quran, 2:180) being abrogated by the hadith: "There is no bequest for inheritors" in Tirmidhī.[7] This is objected to in that the hadith is a solitary report [*āḥād*]; it will come [later] that mass-transmitted reports are not abrogated by solitary reports.

One copy of the basic text [of the *Waraqāt*] includes: "It is not possible for the Sunna to abrogate the Quran, i.e., in contrast to particularization – as preceded – since particularity is of less degree than abrogation."

(ويجوزُ نَسْخُ المتواترِ بالمتواتر، ونسخُ الآحادِ بالآحاد وبالمتواتر).

(ولا يجوزُ نُسْخُ المتواترِ بالآحاد) كالقرآن بالآحاد، لأنه دونه في القوة. والراجح جواز ذلك، لأن محل النسخ هو الحكم والدلالة عليه بالمتواتر ظنية كالآحاد.

It is possible for mass-transmitted reports [*mutawātir*] to abrogate

6 Muslim (977, 1977).
7 Tirmidhī (2120) and others.

mass-transmitted reports, and for solitary reports and mass-transmitted reports to abrogate solitary reports [*āḥād*].

It is not possible for solitary reports to abrogate mass-transmitted reports like the Quran, since solitary reports are inferior to it with respect to strength. However, the preponderant opinion is that it is possible, since the locus of abrogation is the ruling [not the text itself], and the [verse's] signification [of that ruling] conveyed through mass-transmission is probabilistic [*ẓannī*], just like solitary reports.

8

CONFLICTING EVIDENCE

التعارض

(فصل) (وإذا تعارض نطقان فلا يخلو: إمّا أن يكونا عامَّيْنِ، أو خاصَّيْنِ. أو أحدُهما عامًّا والآخر خاصًّا. أو كلٌّ واحد منهما عامًّا من وجه، وخاصًّا من وجه آخر).

When two utterances conflict, it is inescapable that they are either

1. **both of universal applicability;**
2. **both of particular applicability;**
3. **one of them is universal and the other particular; or**
4. **each one of them is universal from one perspective and particular from another.**

(فإن كانا عامَّيْنِ: فإنْ أمكنَ الجمعُ بينهما يُجمعُ) بحمل كل منهما على حال، مثاله حديث «شر الشهود الذي يشهد قبل أن يستشهد»، وحديث «خير الشهود الذي يشهد قبل أن يستشهد» فحمل الأول على ما إذا كان من له الشهادة عالماً بها، والثاني على ما إذا لم يكن عالماً بها، والثاني رواه مسلم بلفظ «ألا أخبركم بخير الشهود الذي يأتي بشهادته قبل أن يسألها». والأول متفق على معناه في حديث «خيركم قرني ثم الذي يلونهم» إلى قوله «ثم يكون بعدهم قوم يشهدون قبل أن يستشهدوا».

If they are both of universal applicability and reconciliation is possible, they are reconciled by applying each one to a [different] circumstance. *Example:* the hadith "the wickedest witnesses are those who bear witness before they are asked to do so," and the hadith "the best witnesses are those who bear witness before being asked to do so." The first hadith is applied to the circumstance where the plaintiff knows that testimony exists, and the second hadith to circumstances where the plaintiff does not. Muslim related the second with the phrase, "Shall I inform you of the best witness of all? He who brings his testimony before it is requested of him."[1] The general meaning of the first hadith is in Bukhārī and Muslim: "The best of you are my generation, then the ones who follow them" – up until where he says, "After them there will be a people who bear witness before they are asked to do so."[2]

(فإن لم يمكنِ الجمعُ بينهما يُتَوَقَّفُ فيهما إنْ لم يُعلمِ التّاريخُ) أي إلى أن يظهر مرجح أحدهما، مثاله قوله تعالى ﴿أَوْ مَا مَلَكَتْ أَيْمَانُهُمْ﴾ وقوله تعالى ﴿وَأَنْ تَجْمَعُوا بَيْنَ الْأُخْتَيْنِ﴾ فالأول يجوز [جمع الأختين] بملك اليمين والثاني يحرم ذلك، فرجح التحريم لأنه أحوط.

If reconciliation between the conflicting evidence is not possible, then one must withhold judgment if their historical order is not known. [Judgment is withheld] until the appearance of something lending preponderance to one [of the two texts]. *Example:* the Quranic verse, *Save for their wives and what their right hand owns* (Quran, 70:30) and, *And [it is forbidden to you] that you should have two sisters together [in marriage]* (Quran, 4:23): since the first permits [having intercourse with two sisters] through slavery while the second prohibits it. Prohibition is preponderant because it is more precautionary.

1 Muslim (1719).
2 Bukhārī (3650) and Muslim (2534).

(فإنْ عُلِمَ التّاريخُ نُسِخَ المتقدَّمُ بالمتأخّر) كما في آيتي عدة الوفاة وآيتي المصابرة وقد تقدمت الأربع.

If their historical order is known, the previous is abrogated by the subsequent. This is what occurred in the two verses concerning the waiting period occasioned by [the husband's] death and the two verses concerning patience. (These four preceded.)

(وكذلك إنْ كانا خاصَّيْنِ) أي فإن أمكن الجمع بينهما جمع كما في حديث «أنه ﷺ توضأ وغسل رجليه» وهذا مشهور في الصحيحين وغيرهما.

وحديث «أنه ﷺ توضأ ورش الماء على قدميه وهما في النعلين» رواه النسائي والبيهقي وغيرهما. فجمع بينهما بأن الرش في حال التجديد لما في بعض الطرق «أن هذا وضوء من لم يحدث».

It is the same if they are both of particular applicability. That is: if reconciliation is possible, they are reconciled. *Example:* the hadith that the Prophet ﷺ made ablution and washed his feet (a well-known report [*mashhūr*] in Bukhārī and Muslim[3]), and the hadith that he ﷺ made ablution and sprinkled water on his feet while they were inside sandals in Nasā'ī, Bayhaqī and others.

The two are reconciled by him ﷺ sprinkling in the situation of repeating [a current] ablution – just as it is in some variant transmissions of the [hadith]: "Verify, this is the ablution of one who did not invalidate it."

وإن لم يمكن الجمع بينهما ولم يعلم التاريخ يتوقف فيهما إلى ظهور مرجح لأحدهما، مثاله ما جاء «أنه ﷺ سئل عما يحل للرجل من امرأته وهي حائض فقال: ما فوق الإزار» رواه أبو داود. وجاء أنه ﷺ قال «اصنعوا كل شيء إلا

3 Bukhārī (1934), and Muslim (226).

النكاح» أي الوطء رواه مسلم. ومن جملته الوطء فيما فوق الإزار. فتعارضا فيه فرجح بعضهم التحريم احتياطاً، وبعضهم الحل لأنه الأصل في المنكوحة.

وإن علم التاريخ نسخ المتقدم بالمتأخر كما تقدم في حديث زيارة القبور.

If combining them is not possible and their historical order is not known, one must abstain [from using either one] until the appearance of something lending one of them preponderance. *Example:* what was conveyed that when the Prophet ﷺ was asked what is permissible for a husband from his wife while she is menstruating, he ﷺ replied: "What lies above the waist-wrapper" narrated by Abū Dāwūd.[4] It is also conveyed that he ﷺ replied, "Do everything except for *nikāḥ*" (i.e., intercourse) in Muslim,[5] which includes [performing the motions of] intercourse above the waist-wrapper, and so the two are in conflict with respect to this intercourse. Some of the scholars consider prohibition preponderant out of caution, while some consider lawfulness preponderant since the default [ruling for intercourse] within wedlock is lawfulness.

If the historical order is known, the previous one is abrogated by the subsequent, just as what preceded in the hadith concerning visiting graves.

(وإنْ كان أحدُهما عامًّا، والآخرُ خاصًّا، فيُخَص العامُّ بالخاصّ) كتخصيص حديث الصحيحين «فيما سقت السماء العشر» بحديثهما «ليس فيما دون خمسة أوسق صدقة» كما تقدم.

If one of the two texts is of universal applicability and the other is of particular applicability, the universal applicability [of one text] is restricted by the particular applicability [of the other text]. *Example:* the hadith in Bukhārī and Muslim: "In everything irrigated by the

4 Abu Dawud (212).
5 Muslim (302).

sky there is [an obligatory *zakāt* of] one tenth,"[6] being restricted by their hadith: "There is no [obligatory] charity [*ṣadaqah*] in anything less than five *awsaq*,"[7] as preceded.

(وإنْ كان كلٌّ منهما عامًّا من وجه، وخاصًّا من وجه، فيُخَصُّ عمومُ كلٍّ منهما بخصوص الآخر) بأن يمكن ذلك، مثاله حديث أبي داود وغيره «إذا بلغ الماء قلتين فإنه لا ينجس» مع حديث ابن ماجة وغيره «الماء لا ينجسه شيء إلا ما غلب على ريحه وطعمه ولونه». فالأول خاص بالقلتين عام في المتغير وغيره. والثاني خاص في المتغير عام في القلتين وما دونها فخص عموم الأول بخصوص الثاني حتى يحكم بأن ماء القلتين ينجس بالتغير وخص عموم الثاني بخصوص الأول حتى يحكم بأن ما دون القلتين ينجس وإن لم يتغير.

If each one of the two texts is of universal applicability from one aspect and of particular applicability from another, then the universal applicability of each one is restricted by the particular applicability of the other if possible. *Example:* the hadith narrated by Abū Dāwūd and others: "When water reaches *qullatayn* [approximately 216 liters], it does not become filthy"[8] with the hadith in Ibn Mājah and others: "Water: nothing renders it filthy except that which overpowers its smell, taste, and color."[9] The first hadith is particular to *qullatayn*, universal with water that is changed and non-changed water; the second hadith is particular to water that is changed, universal concerning *qullatayn* and less. Thus, the universal aspect of the first hadith is restricted by the particular aspect of the second, so it is judged that water measuring *qullatayn* becomes filthy by means of change. And the universal aspect of the second hadith

6 Bukhārī (1483), Muslim (981).
7 Bukhārī (1484), Muslim (979).
8 Abū Dāwūd (63–65), Tirmidhī (67), Nasā'ī (1/46), Aḥmed (2/12), Ḥākim (1/132), Ibn Ḥibbān (2/274–5), Ibn Khuzayma (1/49).
9 Ibn Mājah (521); Bayhaqī has a similar hadith in his *Sunan* (1/260).

is restricted by the particular aspect of the first, so it is ruled that water measuring less than *qullatayn* becomes filthy – even if it did not change.

فإن لم يمكن تخصيص عموم كل منهما بخصوص الآخر احتيج إلى الترجيح بينهما فيما تعارضا فيه مثاله حديث البخاري «من بدل دينه فاقتلوه» وحديث الصحيحين «أنه ﷺ نهى عن قتل النساء» فالأول عام في الرجال والنساء خاص بأهل الردة. والثاني خاص بالنساء عام في الحربيات والمرتدات فتعارضا في المرتدة هل تقتل أم لا؟ [والراجح أنها تقتل]

If it is not possible to restrict each text's universal applicability using the other text's particular applicability, there is a need for something to lend preponderance where the two conflict. *Example:* the hadith in Bukhārī: "Whoever changes his religion: kill him"[10] and the hadith in Bukhārī and Muslim that he ﷺ forbade killing women.[11] The first is universal with respect to men and women, particular with respect to apostates; the second is particular with respect to women, universal with respect to hostile Muslim women and female apostates. Hence, the two conflict with respect to female apostates and whether or not they are killed; the preponderant opinion is that they are.

10 Bukhārī (3017, 6922), Abū Dāwūd (4353), Tirmidhī (1458), Nasā'ī (4059–65).
11 Bukhārī (3014, 3015), Muslim (1744).

9

SCHOLARLY CONSENSUS

الإجماع

(باب) (وأمّا الإجماع فهو اتّفاقُ علماء أهل العصر على حكم الحادثة) فلا يعتبر وفاق العوام لهم. (ونعني بالعلماء الفقهاءَ) فلا يعتبر موافقة الأصوليين لهم، (ونعني بالحادثة الحادثةَ الشّرعيّة) لأنها محل نظر الفقهاء بخلاف اللغوية مثلاً، فإنما يجمع فيها علماء اللغة.

Scholarly consensus [*ijmaʿ*] **is [when] the scholars of an era agree upon the ruling of an actual or potential issue.** Hence, laymen agreeing with them is of no consequence. **By "scholars" we mean the jurists** [***fuqahā***]. And so, scholars of the methodology of jurisprudence [*uṣūliyyūn*] (Ibn Qāsim: who are not jurists) agreeing with them is of no consequence. **By "new issue" we mean a new legal issue** since this is the focus for jurists. [This is] in contrast to linguistic issues – for example – since linguists form consensus concerning linguistic issues.

The Binding Legal Value of Consensus

(وإجماع هذه الأمّة حجّةٌ دون غيرها، لقوله ﷺ: «لاَ تَجْتَمِعُ أُمَّتِي عَلَى ضَلاَلَةٍ») رواه الترمذي وغيره. (والشّرعُ ورد بعصمة الأمّة) لهذا الحديث ونحوه. (والإجماعُ حجّةٌ على العصر الثّاني) ومن بعده، (وفي أيّ عصر كان) من عصر الصحابة ومن بعدهم.

The consensus of the Muslim community is binding [***ḥujja***] **– but not that of other communities. This is because he (May Allah bless**

him and give him peace) said, "My community will not come to consensus over a misguidance", narrated by Tirmidhī and others.[1] **The Legislation conveyed this community's protection** because of this hadith and its like.

Consensus is binding over the next generation and subsequent generations, **no matter in which generation it takes place** including the generation of the Companions (May Allah be pleased with him) and those after them.

(ولا يُشترطُ في حُجِّيَّتِهِ انقراضُ العصر) بأن يموت أهله ([على الصحيح]) لسكوت أدلة الحجية عنه. وقيل يشترط، لجواز أن يطرأ لبعضهم ما يخالف اجتهاده فيرجع عنه. وأجيب بأنه لا يجوز له الرجوع عنه، لإجماعهم عليه.

(فإن قلنا: إنَّ انقراضَ العصرِ شرطٌ، يُعتبرْ) في انعقاد الإجماع (قولُ من ولد في حياتهم، وتفقّه، وصار من أهل الاجتهاد. ولهم [على هذا القول] أن يرجعوا عن ذلك الحكم) الذي أدى اجتهادهم إليه.

In order for it to be binding, it is not a condition that the [entire] generation pass away [that is:] by those in that generation who are qualified [in matters of consensus] dying while they are [gathered in consensus] over the sound opinion. This is because the evidence supporting consensus was silent concerning this condition.

There is an opinion that the entire generation passing away is a condition, because of the possibility that something might occur to one of them which conflicts with his *ijtihād*, and thus he recants it. I reply [to this opinion] that it is not permissible for him to recant it due to their consensus concerning it.

If we were to say that the generation passing away is a condition, then

1 Tirmidhi (2167), Ibn Mājah (4085), Ḥākim (394–9), Abū Dāwūd (4253).

the opinion of someone who was born during their lifetime, became a legist and qualified to make personal reasoning would be of consideration in the consensus taking place; and according to this opinion, **they are entitled to recant that ruling** that their consensus led to.

(والإجماعُ يصحُّ بقولهم وبفعلهم) كأن يقولوا بجواز شيء أو يفعلوه فيدل فعلهم له على جوازه لعصمتهم كما تقدم، (وبقول البعض وبفعل البعض، وانتشار ذلك القول أو الفعل، وسكوت الباقين عليه) ويسمى ذلك بالإجماع السكوتي.

Consensus is valid by means of their words and their deeds (e.g., their saying that something is permissible, or their performing it). This is because their performance indicates its permissibility due to their being protected [from misguidance], just as preceded. **[Consensus is valid] by the statements and deeds of [just] some of them, when that statement or deed spreads while the remainder keeps silent.** This is known as "unvoiced consensus" [*ijmāʿ sukūtī*].

(وقولُ الواحدِ من الصّحابة ليس حجّة على غيره، على القول الجديد) [وفي القديم حجة] لحديث «أصحابي كالنجوم بأيهم اقتديتم اهتديتم»، وأجيب بضعفه.

The opinion of a single Companion (God be well pleased with them all) is not a binding proof over anyone else, according to [Imam al-Shāfiʿī's] new school. In [Imam al-Shāfiʿī's] old school it is a binding proof, because of the hadith "My Companions are like the stars: whichever one you follow, you will be guided." I answer [them saying] that it (trans.: the hadith or opinion) is weak.

10

DECLARATIVE STATEMENTS AND REPORTS

الاخبار

(باب) (وأمّا الأخبار: فالخبرُ ما يدخلُه الصّدقُ والكذبُ) لاحتمالِه لهما من حيث إنه خبر كقولك قام زيد يحتمل أن يكون صدقاً وأن يكون كذباً.

وقد يقطع بصدقه أو كذبه لأمر خارجي. الأول كخبر الله تعالى. والثاني كقولك الضدان يجتمعان.

A declarative statement [*khabr*] is a statement wherein truth and falsehood enter because it bears the possibility (trans.: in theory, as he clarifies in the next paragraph) of them both in that it is a declarative, like saying "Zaid stood" bears the possibility that it is true, and that it is false.

The truth or falsehood of the statement may be unquestionable because of something extrinsic, but not in and of itself. The first [unquestionably true] is like the declaratives of God; the second [unquestionably false] is like saying that "contraries can occur together."

(والخبرُ ينقسمُ إلى آحاد، ومتواتر).

Declarative statements are divided into solitary [*āḥād*] and mass-transmitted [*mutawātir*] reports.

Mass-Transmitted and Solitary Reports

(فصل) (فالمتواترُ ما يوجبُ العلمَ، وهو: أنْ يرويَهُ جماعةٌ، لا يقع التّواطؤُ على الكذب عن مثلهم، إلى أنْ ينتهيَ إلى المخبَرِ عنه، فيكون في الأصل عَنْ مشاهدةٍ أو سماع، لا عنِ اجتهادٍ) كالإخبار عن مشاهدة مكة أو سماع خبر الله تعالى من النبي ﷺ، بخلاف الإخبار عن مجتهد فيه كإخبار الفلاسفة بقدم العالم.

Mass-transmitted [*mutawātir*] reports are those that necessarily convey sure knowledge [*'ilm*]. A mass-transmitted report is that which has been related by a group the likes of which cannot simultaneously agree upon a lie, from a similar group, [and so on,] up until the thing being reported; and the thing being reported being something observed or heard – not personal reasoning. *Example:* reports of seeing Mecca and hearing reports from God via the Prophet ﷺ. This is in contrast to reports of something arrived at through personal reasoning. For *example:* philosophers declaring the world to be without beginning).

(والآحادُ) وهو مقابل المتواتر (هو: الذي يوجبُ العملَ، ولا يوجبُ العلمَ، لاحتمال الخطأ فيه).

Solitary reports [*āḥād*] – in contrast to mass-transmitted reports – **are those that necessarily lead to performance but do not necessarily convey sure knowledge [*'ilm*] because of bearing the possibility of it being a mistake.**

Expedient and Grounded Reports

(فصل) (وينقسمُ إلى قسمين: إلى مرسل ومسند).

(فالمسندُ: ما اتّصل إسنادُه) بأن صرح برواته كلهم، (والمرسلُ: ما لم يتّصل إسنادُه) بأن أسقط بعض رواته.

Reports divide into two divisions: *expedient,* and *grounded.*

***Grounded reports* [*musnad*] are those possessing a continuously connected chain of transmitters [*sanad*]** through explicit mention of all of its transmitters.

(فإنْ كان من مَراسيلَ غير الصّحابة فليس بحجّةٍ) لاحتمال أن يكون الساقط مجروحاً، (إلاّ مراسيلَ سعيدِ بنِ المُسَيَّبِ) من التابعين أسقط الصحابي وعزاها للنبي ﷺ فهي حجة، (فإنها فُتِّشَتْ) أي فتش عنها (فَوُجِدَتْ مسانيدَ) أي رواها له (الصّحابيّ) الذي أسقطه (عن النّبيّ ﷺ) وهو في الغالب صهره أبو زوجته أبو هريرة رضي الله عنه.

أما مراسيل الصحابة بأن يروي صحابي عن صحابي عن النبي ﷺ ثم يسقط الثاني، فحجة لأن الصحابة كلهم عدول.

***Expedient reports* [*mursal*] are those lacking a continuously connected chain** through some of its transmitters being omitted. **If the expedient report is not from one of the Companions (God be well pleased with them), it is not a binding proof** because it bears the possibility of the omitted reporter being discredited – **unless it is an expedient report from Saʿīd bin al-Musayyab (May Allah be pleased with him),** a Successor [*tābiʿīn*], where he omitted the Companion (May Allah be pleased with him) and ascribed it to the Prophet ﷺ – it is a binding proof, **since his reports have been examined** and [exhaustively] searched, **and grounded chains of transmission were found** to the Prophet ﷺ, related to him through the Companion (May Allah be pleased with him) whom he omitted; most of them being [through] his father-in-law Abū Hurayra (May Allah be pleased with him).

As for *expedient reports* transmitted by Companions (May Allah be pleased with them) by which one Companion relates from another Companion from the Prophet ﷺ, and the second Companion is omitted [from the chain]: it is a binding proof because all of the Companions (May Allah be pleased with them) are upright.

(والعَنْعَنَةُ) بأن يقال حدثنا فلان عن فلان إلى آخره (تدخل على الإسناد) أي على حكمه فيكون الحديث المروي بها في حكم المسند، [لا المرسل] لاتصال سنده في الظاهر.

[Reports using] ***indecisive hadith transmission*** **terminology [*'an'ana*]** by which one says: so-and-so reported from so-and-so, and so forth up until the end [of the chain] **enter into grounded reports.** That is: they are judged to be the same. Thus, hadiths related using indecisive terminology come under the ruling of grounded reports – not under the ruling of expedient reports – because the chain's outward appearance is continuity.

(وإذا قرأ الشَّيخُ يجوزُ للرّاوي أن يقولَ: «حَدَّثَنِي» أو «أَخْبَرَنِي». وإنْ قرأ هو على الشّيخ فيقولُ: «أَخْبَرَنِي» ولا يقول: «حَدَّثَنِي») لأنه لم يحدثه. ومنهم من أجاز حدثني وعليه عرف أهل الحديث لأن القصد الإعلام بالرواية عن الشيخ.

When the shaykh reads while someone else listens, **it is permissible for the transmitter to say: "he related to me" [*ḥaddathanī*], or: "he informed me" [*akhbaranī*]. When he reads to the shaykh, he says: "he informed me," but does not say: "he related to me."** [He says this] since the shaykh did not relate to him. Some permitted [him to say:] "he related to me" – the custom of Ahl al-Ḥadīth [the Folk of Ḥadīth] follows this – since the goal is announcing transmission from the shaykh.

(وإنْ أجازَهُ الشّيخُ من غير قراءة فيقول الرّاوي: «أَجَازَنِي» أو «أَخْبَرَنِي إِجَازَةً».)

If the shaykh authorizes him without reading, the transmitter says: "he authorized me," or: "he informed me through an authorization."

11

ANALOGICAL REASONING

القياس

(باب) (وأمّا القياسُ فهو ردُّ الفرعِ إلى الأصل بعلّة تجمعُهما في الحكم) كقياس الأرز على البر [في الربا] بجامع الطعم.

Analogical reasoning is returning a derived case [*far'*] back to the original case [*aṣl*] due to an apparent cause [*'illah*] that joins them in the ruling. For *example:* rice being analogous to wheat with regards to interest, as they are linked in that they are both edible.

Divisions of Analogical Reasoning

(فصل) (وهو ينقسم إلى ثلاثة أقسام: إلى قياس علّة، وقياس دلالة، وقياس شَبَهٍ.)

(فقياسُ علّةٍ ما كانت العلّةُ فيه موجبةً للحكم) بحيث لا يحسن عقلاً تخلفه عنها كقياس الضرب على التأفيف للوالدين في التحريم بعلة الإيذاء.

Analogical reasoning divides into three divisions: *causative, indicative,* and *similitude.*

***Causative analogy* [*qiyās al-'illah*] is that in which the apparent cause [*'illah*] necessarily requires the ruling** whereby it does not seem sound – rationally – for it to deviate from it. *Example:* beating being analogous to saying "Fie!" to one's parents with respect to it being unlawful, because of the apparent cause of harm.

(وقياسُ الدّلالةِ هو الاستدلالُ بأحد النّظيرَيْنِ على الآخر. وهو أنْ تكونَ العلّةُ دالّةً على الحكم، ولا تكون موجبةً للحكم) كقياس مال الصبي على مال البالغ في وجوب الزكاة فيه بجامع أنه مال نام. ويجوز أن يقال لا تجب في مال الصبي كما قال به أبو حنيفة.

***Indicative analogy* [*qiyās al-dalālah*] is using one of two identical things as evidence for the other. It is when the apparent cause [*'illah*] indicates the ruling without necessarily requiring the ruling.** *Example:* a youth's property is analogous to a mature person's property, in it being obligatory to pay *zakāt* from it because they are joined in being [susceptible] to growth. It is possible to say that *zakāt* is not obligatory with respect to a youth's property, just as Abu Ḥanīfa said concerning it.

(وقياسُ الشَّبَهِ هو الفَرْعُ المُتَرَدّدُ بين أصلَيْنِ، فيلحقُ بأكثرِهما شبهًا به) كما في العبد إذا أتلف فإنه متردد في الضمان بين الإنسان الحر من حيث أنه آدمي، وبين البهيمة من حيث أنه مال، وهو بالمال أكثر شبهاً من الحر، بدليل أنه يباع ويورث ويوقف وتضمن أجزاؤه بما نقص من قيمته.

***Analogy of similitude* [*qiyās al-shabah*] is when the derived case resembles two source cases, so it is attached to whichever one it most resembles.** *Example:* [recompense for] a damaged slave, since with respect to the recompense there is indecision [as to] whether he is [analogous to] a free human – from the perspective that he is a human – or an animal – from the perspective that he is property. He resembles property more than he resembles a free human, through the proof that he is sold, can be inherited or declared an endowment, and there is recompense for his components [when damaged] in proportion to what they [when damaged] reduce from his sale value [when complete].

Conditions for the Integrals of Analogical Reasoning

(فصل) (ومن شرط الفَرْعِ أَنْ يكونَ مناسبًا للأصل) فيما يجمع به بينهما للحكم، [أي أن يجمع بينهما بمناسب للحكم].

A condition of the derived case is that it be appropriate to the original case. [This is] with respect to what links the two together for the ruling, meaning that something join between them that is appropriate for the ruling.

(ومن شرط الأصل أَنْ يكونَ ثابتًا بدليل مُتّفَق عليه بين الخصمَيْن) ليكون القياس حجة على الخصم. فإن لم يكن خصم فالشرط ثبوت حكم الأصل بدليل يقول به القيّاس.

A condition of the original case is that it is established through evidence that is agreed upon by the debating parties so that the analogy is binding over the debating party. If there is no debating party, then the condition is that the ruling of the original case be established by evidence that the one making the analogy [himself] considered authoritative.

(ومن شرط العلّة أَنْ تَطَّرِدَ في معلولاتها، فلا تَنْتَقِضُ لفظًا، ولا معنىً) فمتى انتقضت لفظاً بأن صدقت الأوصاف المعبر بها عنها في صورة بدون الحكم أو معنى بأن وجد المعنى المعلل به في صورة بدون الحكم فسد القياس. الأول كأن يقال في القتل بمثقل أنه قتل عمد عدوان، فيجب به القصاص، كالقتل بالمحدد، فينتقض ذلك بقتل الوالد ولده فإنه لا يجب به قصاص. والثاني كأن يقال تجب الزكاة في المواشي لدفع حاجة الفقير، فيقال ينتقض ذلك بوجوده في الجواهر ولا زكاة فيها.

A condition of the apparent cause [*'illah*] is that it is constant in the rulings wherein it exists, so that it not be inconsistent in phrase or meaning. The analogy is invalid whenever the apparent cause is

1. inconsistent in phrase (by it holding true for the characteristics which are an indication of the apparent cause [*'illah*] in one scenario, but not the ruling); or
2. [inconsistent in] meaning (by the meaning of the apparent cause [*'illah*] existing in one scenario – but not its ruling).

The first [*inconsistent in phrase*] is like saying that killing using a blunt instrument is premeditated murder [*qatl 'amd 'udwān*], and so reciprocal retaliation [*qiṣāṣ*] is obligatory, just like killing with a sharp instrument. This is rendered inconsistent by the scenario where a father kills his son, since it does not obligate reciprocal retaliation.

The second [*inconsistent in meaning*] is like saying that *zakāt* is obligatory for livestock in order to alleviate the needs of the poor. This is rendered inconsistent by [the same apparent cause (*'illah*): alleviating the needs of the poor via *zakāt*] existing in jewels, while there is no *zakāt* for them.

(ومن شرط الحكم أنْ يكونَ مثلَ العلّة في النّفي والإثبات) أي تابعاً لها. في ذلك [إن وجدت] وجد وإن انتفت انتفى.

A condition of the ruling [*ḥukm*] is that it be similar to the apparent cause [*'illah*] with regard to absence and presence i.e., following the apparent cause in this: when the apparent cause is present, the ruling is present; when the apparent cause is absent, the ruling is absent.

(والعلّةُ هي الجالبةُ للحكم) بمناسبتها له (والحكمُ هو المجلوبُ للعلّة) لما ذكر.

The apparent cause [*'illah*] **is what attracts the ruling** due to the apparent cause being appropriate for the ruling**, and the ruling is that which is attracted by the apparent cause** because of what was mentioned.

12

PROHIBITION AND PERMISSIBILITY

الحظر والإباحة

(فصل) (وأمّا الحظرُ والإباحةُ: فمن النّاس من يقولُ: إنّ الأشياءَ) بعد البعثة (على الحظر، إلاّ ما أباحته الشّريعةُ. فإن لم يوجدْ في الشّريعة ما يدلُّ على الإباحة فيُسْتَمْسَكُ بالأصل، وهو الحظرُ) أي على صفة هي الحظر، إلا ما أباحته الشريعة، فإن لم يوجد في الشريعة ما يدل على الإباحة، يتمسك بالأصل وهو الحظر.

As for impermissibility and permissibility: some scholars say that things after the Prophet (May Allah bless him and give him peace) was appointed to spread Islam [*al-bi'tha*] **are impermissible** (i.e., upon an attribute which is being impermissible) **unless the Legislation declares it permissible. And so, if nothing in the Legislation is found that indicates permissibility, one adheres to the original state – impermissibility.**

(ومن النّاس من يقولُ بضدّه، وهو أنّ الأصلَ في الأشياء) بعد البعثة أنها على (الإباحةُ، إلاّ ما حظره الشّرعُ).

Some scholars hold the opposite: that the default state for things after the Prophet ﷺ was appointed [*al-bi'thah*] **is the opposite [permissibility], except for what the Legislation has declared impermissible.**

والصحيح التفصيل، [وهو أن] المضار على التحريم، والمنافع على الحل.

أما قبل البعثة فلا حكم يتعلق بأحد، لانتفاء الرسول الموصل إليه.

The sound opinion is that it is contextual: harmful things are unlawful, beneficial things are lawful.

As for before the Prophet ﷺ was appointed [*al-bi'thah*], no ruling is associated with anyone because of the absence of the messenger to bring him the ruling.

13

PRESUMPTION OF CONTINUITY

استصحاب الحال

(فصل) (ومعنى استصحاب الحال) الذي يحتج به كما سيأتي: (أنْ يُسْتَصْحَبَ الأصلُ) أي العدم الأصلي (عند عدم الدّليل الشّرعيّ) بأن لم يجده المجتهد بعد البحث عنه بقدر الطاقة كأن لم يجد دليلاً على وجوب صوم رجب فيقول لا يجب باستصحاب الحال أي [العدم الأصلي] وهو حجة جزماً.

The meaning of "presumption of continuity" [***istiṣḥāb al-ḥāl***] that is cited as binding, as will come, **is that the original state** (i.e., the default of [the ruling's] absence) **is presumed to continue in the absence of legal evidence** by the *mujtahid* not finding any after intensively searching for it, as much as able. It is like [the *mujtahid*] not finding evidence indicating that fasting the month of Rajab is obligatory, so he says that it is not obligatory out of presuming continuity, i.e., the default of [the ruling's] absence. It is binding, with certainty.

أما الاستصحاب المشهور، الذي هو ثبوت أمر في الزمن الثاني لثبوته في الأول فحجة عندنا دون الحنفية فلا زكاة عندنا في عشرين ديناراً ناقصة تروج رواج الكاملة بالاستصحاب.

As for the presumption of continuity that is well known (which is asserting something at a later time because of its assertion at a previous time): it is binding in our opinion, but not according to the Ḥanafis. Thus, in our opinion there is no *zakāt* owed on twenty defective *dīnār*s that circulate [as] twenty whole *dīnār*s, because of the presumption of continuity [of the default of no *zakāt* being owed].

14

THE ORDER OF PRECEDENCE IN WHICH EVIDENCE IS CITED

ترتيب الأدلّة

(باب) (وأمّا الأدلّةُ فيتقدّمُ الجَليُّ منها على الخفيّ) وذلك كالظاهر والمؤول فيقدم اللفظ في معناه الحقيقي على معناه المجظازي.

Manifest evidence is given precedence over the hidden. That is: evident and interpreted. So, the phrase's literal meaning is given precedence over its figurative meaning.

(والموجبُ للعلم على الموجب للظّنِّ) وذلك كالمتواتر والآحاد فيقدم الأول إلا أن يكون عاماً فيخص بالثاني كما تقدم من تخصيص الكتاب بالسنة.

Evidence that necessarily leads to sure knowledge [*'ilm*] is given precedence over evidence which leads to probable knowledge [*ẓann*]. That is like mass-transmitted reports and solitarily-transmitted reports. So, the first is given precedence unless it is universally applicable, in which case it is rendered particular by the second – just as what preceded of the Quran being rendered particular by the Sunna.

(والنّطقُ) من كتاب أو سنة (على القياس)، إلا أن يكون النطق عاماً، فيخص بالقياس كما تقدم.

Something stated from the Quran and Sunna **is given precedence over analogical reasoning.** That is: unless what is stated categorically is of universal applicability; it is then rendered particular by analogy (as has preceded).

(والقياسُ الجَلِيِّ على الخفي) وذلك كقياس العلة على قياس الشبه.

Manifest analogical reasoning [*qiyās jalī*] is given precedence over concealed analogical reasoning [*qiyās khafī*]. Similarly: a causative analogy [*qiyās al-ʿillah*] takes precedence over an analogy of similitude [*qiyās al-shabah*].

(فإنْ وُجد في النّطق) من كتاب أو سنة (ما يغيِّر الأصْل) أي العدم الأصلي الذي يعبر عن استصحابه باستصحاب الحال فواضح أنه يعمل بالنطق، (وإلاّ) وإن لم يوجد ذلك (فيُستصحبُ الحالُ) أي العدم الأصلي أي يعمل به.

If something from the Quran or Sunna [that is] **stated categorically is found to change the default state** (the default of absence, which when presumed to continue is expressed as "presumption of continuity" [*istiṣḥāb al-ḥāl*]), it is clear that the categorically stated phrases are used. **Otherwise** (if it is not found), **the original state is presumed to continue [*istiṣḥāb al-ḥāl*].** That is: its default of absence; and it is acted in accordance to it.

15

THE MUFTI, HIS PETITIONER & EMULATION

المفتي والمستفتي والتقليد

The Muftī

(فصل) (ومن شرط المفتي) وهو المجتهد (أنْ يكونَ عالمًا بالفقه: أصلًا وفرعًا خلافًا ومذهبًا) أي بمسائل الفقه، وقواعده وفروعه، وبما فيها من الخلاف، ليذهب إلى قول منه ولا يخالفه، بأن يحدث قولاً آخر، لاستلزام اتفاق من قبله بعدم ذهابهم إليه [على نفيه] (وأنْ يكونَ كاملَ الآلةِ في الاجتهاد، عارفًا بما يحتاجُ إليه في استنباط الأحكام: من النّحو، واللّغة، ومعرفة الرّجال الرّاوين) ليأخذ برواية المقبول منهم دون المجروح، (وتفسيرِ الآياتِ الواردةِ في الأحكام، والأخبارِ الواردةِ فيها) ليوافق ذلك في اجتهاده ولا يخالفه.

Conditions of the *muftī* who is the *mujtahid* include

1. **Being knowledgeable in *fiqh* – its foundations and branches – in the differences of opinion and the school's position.** This includes [being knowledgeable] in legal issues, its foundational rules, and its branches. [It includes being knowledgeable in] the differences of opinions therein, so that he takes one of these opinions and does not go against them by inventing a different opinion. This is due to him being required to conform to his predecessors; and since their absence of taking that opinion negates it as a possibility.
2. **Being versed in the tools necessary for *ijtihād* by knowing what is needed to deduce rulings, including Arabic grammar and**

lexicography.

3. **Being versed in narrators** of reports. This is so that he takes from the accounts of those who are accepted, not from the discredited.
4. **Being versed in the commentaries of Quranic verses and prophetic hadiths concerning rulings.** This is so that he agrees with them in his *ijtihād* and not disagree with them.

وما ذكره من قوله عارفاً إلى آخره من جملة آلة الاجتهاد.

What he mentioned after "being versed in the tools" is part of the mass of evidence used for *ijtihād*.

ومنها معرفته بقواعد الأصول وغير ذلك.

A condition for the *muftī* is that he knows the fundamentals of jurisprudence, and other things (trans.: e.g., specific issues where consensus has occurred, and specific issues where scholars disagree and the range of their disagreement).

The Petitioner

(فصل) (ومن شرط المستفتِي أنْ يكونَ من أهل التّقليد، فيقلِّدُ المفتيَ في الفُتيا) لم يكن الشخص من أهل التقليد بأن كان من أهل الاجتهاد فليس له أن يستفتي كما قال، (وليس للعالِم أنْ يقلِّدَ) لتمكنه من الاجتهاد.

A condition of the one petitioning the *muftī* [*al-mustaftī*] is being from those who imitate scholars, so he follows the *muftī* in his verdict.

If the individual is not among those qualified to imitate – by him being one of those qualified to make *ijtihād* – then he is not entitled to petition a *muftī*, just as the author said: **It is not permissible for**

a scholar (i.e., a *mujtahid*) **to imitate** since he possesses the wherewithal to perform *ijtihād*.

Imitating

(فصل) (والتّقليدُ قبولُ قَوْلِ القائلِ بلا حجّة) يذكرها. (فعلى هذا قبولُ قول النّبيّ ﷺ) فيما يذكره من الأحكام (يُسمَّى تقليدًا).

Imitating [*taqlīd*] is accepting another's opinion without him mentioning **its proof. Consequently, accepting the opinion of the Prophet** ﷺ in the rulings that he mentioned **is called "imitation".**

(ومنهم من قال: التّقليدُ قبولُ قولِ القائلِ، وأنت لا تدري من أين قاله) أي لا تعلم مأخذه في ذلك.

Some said that imitation is to accept another's opinion while you do not know from where he took it (i.e., how he arrived at it).

(فإن قلنا: إنّ النّبيّ ﷺ كان يقولُ بالقياس فيجوزُ أنْ يُسمّى قبولُ قوله تقليدًا) لاحتمال أن يكون عن اجتهاد. وإن قلنا إنه لا يجتهد وإنما يقول عن وحي ﴿ وَمَا يَنطِقُ عَنِ الْهَوَىٰ ۞ إِنْ هُوَ إِلَّا وَحْيٌ يُوحَىٰ﴾ فلا يسمى قبول قوله تقليداً، لاستناده إلى الوحي.

If we hold the opinion that the Prophet (may Allah bless him and give him peace) gave rulings based on analogical reasoning by exercising *ijtihād*, **then it is permissible to call accepting his opinion imitation.** This is because it is possible that the opinion of the Prophet ﷺ was based on *ijtihād*. If we hold the opinion that he ﷺ did not exercise *ijtihād* but only said things based upon Revelation and [with the verse] *Nor does he speak out of passion, This is but a Revelation* *that is revealed* (Quran, 53:3–4), then accepting his opinion is not considered imitation as it rests on Revelation.

16

PERSONAL REASONING

الاجتهاد

(فصل) (وأمّا الاجتهادُ فهو بَذْلُ الوُسْعِ في بلوغ الغرض) المقصود من العلم ليحصل له.

(فالمجتهدُ إن كان كاملَ الآلةِ في الاجتهاد) كما تقدم: (فإنِ اجتهدَ في الفُرُوع فأصاب، فله أجران) على اجتهاده وإصابته؛ (وإنِ اجتهد فيها وأخطأ، فله أجرٌ) واحد على اجتهاده وسيأتي دليل ذلك.

***Ijtihād* ["personal reasoning"] is expending all efforts in reaching the goal** that is the purpose of knowledge, so that he [the *mujtahid*] achieves it. **When a *mujtahid* exercises independent reasoning in branch issues and he has complete [mastery of the] tools for independent reasoning** (as preceded) **and he hits the mark – he has two rewards** – for his personal reasoning and for hitting the mark; **if he exercises independent reasoning and misses then he has one** single reward – for his personal reasoning (the evidence is forthcoming).

(ومنهم من قال: كلُّ مجتهدٍ في الفروع مُصيبٌ) بناءاً على أن حكم الله تعالى في حقه وحق مقلده ما أدى إليه اجتهاده.

Some scholars held the opinion that every *mujtahid* in derived issues hits the mark. This is based upon the ruling of God [deduced by him] with respect to him and the one who imitates him being whatever his personal reasoning led to.

(ولا يجوزُ أنْ يقالَ: كلُّ مجتهدٍ في الأصول الكلاميّة) أي العقائد (مصيبٌ، لأنّ ذلك يؤدّي إلى تصويب أهل الضّلالة من النّصارى) في قولهم بالتثليث (والمجوس) في قولهم بالأصلين للعالم النور والظلمة (والكفّار) في نفيهم التوحيد وبعثة الرسل والمعاد في الآخرة (والملحدين) في نفيهم صفاته تعالى كالكلام وخلقه أفعال العباد وكونه مرئياً في الآخرة وغير ذلك.

It is not possible to hold the opinion that every *mujtahid* in root theological issues (beliefs) hits the mark since it would lead to declaring those who are misguided [e.g.,] **Christians** because of their opinion regarding the Trinity, **Zoroastrians** because of their opinion of the dualistic nature of existence: light and darkness, **non-believers** in their negation of monotheism, the Prophet ﷺ being delegated as a prophet, and the resurrection in the Afterlife, **and atheists** in their negation of the attributes of God, such as His speech, creating the actions of His devotees, that He will be seen in the Afterlife, and others, **as hitting the mark.**

(ودليلُ مَن قال: ليس كلُّ مجتهد في الفروع مصيبًا قولُهُ ﷺ: «مَنِ اجْتَهَدَ فَأَصَابَ فَلَهُ أَجْرَانِ وَمَنِ اجْتَهَدَ وَأَخْطَأَ فَلَهُ أَجْرٌ وَاحِدٌ»، وجه الدليل أنّ النّبيّ ﷺ خطّأ المجتهدَ تارةً وصوّبه أُخرى) والحديث رواه الشيخان ولفظ البخاري: «إذا اجتهد الحاكم فحكم فأصاب فله أجران وإذا حكم فأخطأ فله أجر».

The evidence for those who say that every *mujtahid* does not [always] hit the mark is the saying of the Prophet ﷺ: "Whoever exercises independent reasoning and hits the mark gets two rewards, and whoever exercises independent reasoning and misses gets one reward." The reasoning is that the Prophet ﷺ declared some *mujtahid*s missing the mark sometimes, and declared them hitting it in others. And the hadith which is in Bukhārī and Muslim that – using Bukhārī's wording – "The judge exercises personal reasoning: if he passes judgment and hits the mark he gets two rewards; if he passes judgment and is wrong, he has one reward."[1]

(والله أعلم)

And God knows best.

1 Bukhārī (7352) and Muslim (1716).

APPENDIX A

BASIC TEXT OF THE WARAQĀT

متن الورقات

AUTHOR'S INTRODUCTION

In the name of God, the Merciful and Compassionate

These pages include some of the topics of jurisprudence [*uṣūl al-fiqh*].

The Meanings Of "base," "branch," and "understanding"

[*Uṣūl al-fiqh*] is composed of two individual components.

The word "base" [*aṣl*] is a thing upon which another thing is built.

The word "branch" [*far'*] is a thing that is built upon another thing.

The word "law" [*fiqh*] is knowing legal rulings which are reached through *ijtihād* [qualified reasoning].

Categories of Rulings

There are seven rulings:

1. obligation [*wājib*];
2. recommended [*mandūb*];
3. neutral [*mubāḥ*];
4. forbidden [*maḥẓūr*];
5. offensive [*makrūh*];

6. valid [*ṣaḥīḥ*];
7. invalid [*bāṭil*].

Obligation is anything for which one is rewarded if performed and punished if omitted.

Recommended is anything for which one is rewarded for if performed, yet not punished if omitted.

Neutral is anything for which one is neither rewarded for if performed, nor punished for if omitted.

Forbidden is anything for which one is rewarded if omitted and punished if performed.

Offensive is anything for which one is rewarded if omitted yet not punished if performed.

Valid is that to which being effective and of legal significance pertain.

Invalid is that to which being effective and of legal significance do not pertain.

Clarifying the meanings of knowledge, suspicion, and doubt

Fiqh is more constrained than knowledge [*'ilm*]. The word "*'ilm*" [means] knowing that which is known as it is in reality.

Ignorance [*jahl*] is conceptualizing something contrary to as it is in reality.

Compulsory knowledge [*al-'ilm al-ḍarūrī*] is that which does not depend on pondering and inference.

Acquired knowledge [*al-'ilm al-muktasab*] depends on pondering and inference

Pondering [*naẓr*] is contemplating the state of the object of contemplation.

Inference [*istididlāl*] is seeking evidence [*al-dalīl*].

Evidence [*al-dalīl*] is what guides to that which is being sought.

Probable [*ẓann*] is when two matters are possible, with one being more apparent than the other.

Doubt [*shakk*] is when two matters are possible, while neither possesses a feature distinguishing it over the other.

The Meaning of Jurisprudence

The bases of law [*uṣūl al-fiqh*] are its ways, in general and in the manner in which they are used for inference.

The Topics of Jurisprudence

The topics of jurisprudence are:

- categories of phrases [*aqsām al-kalām*];
- commands and prohibitions [*al-amr wa al-nahī*];
- universal and particular applicability [*al-'āmm wa al-khāṣṣ*];
- ambiguity and clarification [*al-mujmal wa al-mubayyan*];
- evident [*al-ẓāhir*];
- actions of the Prophet [*al-af'āl*];
- the abrogating and the abrogated [*al-nāsikh wa al-mansūkh*];
- scholarly consensus [*al-ijma'*];
- declarative statements and reports [*al-akhbār*];
- analogical reasoning [*al-qiyās*];
- prohibition and permissibility [*al-ḥaẓr wa al-ibūḥah*];
- the order of precedence in which evidence is cited [*tartīb al-adillah*];
- the attributes of those who give legal edicts and their petitioners [*ṣifāt al-muftī wa al-mustaftī*]; and

- rulings pertaining to personal reasoning [*aḥkām al-mujtahidīn*]

CATEGORIES OF PHRASES

The bare minimums from which a phrase can be composed are:

- two nouns;
- one noun and one verb;
- one verb and one particle; and
- one noun and one particle

Phrases divide into:

- commands and prohibitions;
- declaratives; and
- interrogatives

Phrases also divide into:

- fancy [*tamanin*];
- urging [*ʿaraḍ*]; and
- oaths [*qasam*].

Clarifying Literal and Figurative

From another perspective, phrases divide into:

- literal; and
- figurative.

Literal [*al-ḥaqīqah*] is that whose usage remains according to its original meaning [*mawḍūʿ*]; or [a second definition]: that which is used according to the convention of its audience.

Figurative [*al-majāz*] is that which has exceeded its conventional meaning.

Literal phrases are either:

- linguistic;
- legal; or
- conventional.

Figurative is by means of either:

- addition [*ziyādah*];
- deletion [*naqṣān*];
- transfer [*naql*]; or
- borrowing [*isti'ārah*].

Figurative by addition is like the Quranic verse, *Nothing like* [kāf] *what is identical* [mithl] *unto Him* (Quran, 42:11).

Figurative by deletion is like the Quranic verse, *Ask the village* (Quran, 12:82).

Figurative by transfer is like using the word *ghā'iṭ* for feces.

Figurative by borrowing is like the Quranic verse, ...*A wall wanting to collapse* (Quran, 18:77).

COMMANDS

A command is using an utterance to demand an action from someone who is inferior, in a way that conveys obligation.

The verbal form for conveying commands is *if'al.*

When a command is categorical and free of contextual circumstances, it is interpreted to convey obligation unless there is evidence indicating that what is intended is its recommendedness or its permissibility. [If there is such evidence,] that is how it is interpreted.

A command does not entail repetition, according to the sound position, unless there is evidence indicating that repetition is intended.

Commands do not entail immediacy.

The command to bring about the existence of the action is a command to perform it and everything which it requires in order to be carried out. For example, the command to perform prayer is a command to perform the purification which leads to it.

If the command is performed, the [person] ordered is cleared of the injunction.

Who Commands and Prohibitions Include

Believers enter [within the scope of] the speech of God (Mighty and Majestic is He!).

Those who are forgetful, minors, or insane do not enter into those addressed.

Non-believers are intended recipients of the particulars of Sacred Law and of that which is required for its valid performance – Islam – because of the Quranic verse, *"What led you into the flame?" They will say: "Because we were not of those who prayed..."* (Quran, 74:42–3).

The command to perform something specific is a prohibition from performing its opposite. The prohibition of performing something specific is a command to perform its opposite.

Prohibitions

A prohibition is using an utterance to invite (i.e., request) an action from an inferior, in a way that conveys obligation.

The verbal phrase for commands may be mentioned while what is intended is:

- mere permissibility;
- a threat;
- equality between two things; and
- spontaneous formation.

UNIVERSAL & PARTICULAR APPLICABILITY

Universal applicability [*'āmm*] is what includes two or more things. [It comes] from the phrase "I included Zayd and Omar with the gift," and "I included men in their entirety with the gift".

The phrases are four:

1. nouns made definite using the definite article [*alif-lām*];
2. mass nouns made definite by the definite article;
3. ambiguous nouns, like:
    1. "whoever" for sentient beings,
    2. "whatever" for non-sentient beings,
    3. "whichever" interrogative, conditional, or appositive for them both,
    4. "wherever" for the spatial,
    5. "whenever" for the temporal,
    6. "whatever" for interrogatives,
    7. "whatever" with consequences, and
    8. other things; and
4. the negative with indefinite nouns.

Universal applicability is an attribute of utterances. It is not permissible to claim universal applicability for actions and other things which take their course.

Particular applicability [*al-khāṣṣ*] is opposite to universal applicability.

Particular Applicability

Particularization [*takhṣīṣ*] is distinguishing part of the sentence.

[Phrases for] declaring something particular are divided into connected and disjointed.

Connected particularization includes:

- exceptions;
- conditionals; and
- qualification using an attribute.

Excepting [*istithnā'*] is removing something that otherwise would have been included by the phrase.

Excepting is valid only with the condition that something remains from *that which the exclusion is being made.*

One of its conditions is that it be linked to the phrase.

It is permissible to put *that which is excluded before that from which it is excluded.*

It is permissible to exclude from the [same] category [*jins*] – as was mentioned above – and from other things.

Conditionals are permitted to precede that which is stipulated by it.

[When] something is qualified by an attribute, the unqualified is interpreted as [being similarly] qualified, such as a slave qualified by "belief" in some places – thus the unqualified is interpreted as agreeing with the qualified.

What Can Be Rendered Particular and By What

It is possible for:

- the Quran to be rendered particular by the Quran;
- the Quran to be rendered particular by the *sunna*;
- the *sunna* to be rendered particular by the Quran;
- the *sunna* to be rendered particular by the *sunna*; and
- utterances to be rendered particular by analogical reasoning. By "utterances" we mean the words of God (Mighty and Majestic is He!) and of the Messenger (May Allah bless him and give him peace).

AMBIGUITY & CLARIFICATION

Ambiguity [*mujmal*] is that which is in need of clarification.

Clarification [*al-bayān*] is taking something from the realm of ambiguity into the realm of being evident.

The unequivocal [*naṣṣ*] is that which cannot be interpreted except as having one single meaning; or: whose interpretation is [just] as it was revealed.

[The Arabic technical term *naṣṣ*] is derived from *minaṣṣat al-ʿurūs*, which is the platform.

Evident & Interpreted

Evident [*al-ẓāhir*] is that which can be interpreted in two ways, where one [interpretation] is more preponderant than the other.

Evident [*ẓāhir*] is interpreted if there is evidence. It is called "evident through evidence" [*ẓāhiran bi-l-dalīl*].

ACTIONS OF THE PROPHET ﷺ

The actions of the Legislator ﷺ are either in the manner of acts of worship and obedience, or not.

If they are in the manner of acts of worship and obedience and there is evidence indicating it being particular to him, then it is interpreted as being particular.

If no evidence indicates this, then the action is not particular to him, because of the Quranic verse, *In the messenger of God you have a good example for him who hopes in God and the Last Day, and remembers God much* (Quran, 33:21). [The action] is interpreted as being obligatory according to some of our [Shāfiʿī] colleagues Some of our colleagues opined that one must withhold judgment.

If the action is not in the manner of worship and obedience, then it is interpreted as being merely permissible.

The tacit approval [*iqrār*] of the Legislator ﷺ of a statement is the statement of the Legislator, and his endorsement of an action is just as his [own] action.

The ruling of things done while he ﷺ was alive yet not in his presence, and that he knew of yet did not reject, is the same as something done in his presence [*majlis*].

ABROGATION

The meaning of abrogation [*naskh*] is "to efface." One says, "the sun effaced the shadow" when it removes it. It is also said that it comes from "to transfer," from the saying, "I transferred what was in the book" when he transfers it in the manner in which it was written.

Its definition is a discourse [*khiṭāb*] indicating the subsequent repeal of a ruling established by a previous discourse, in such a way that without which the ruling would remain established.

Divisions of Abrogation

It is possible for:

- the written record to be abrogated while its ruling remains;
- the ruling to be abrogated while its written record remains; and
- both [the written record and its ruling] to be abrogated.

Abrogation is divided into that which has a replacement, and that which does not.

[Abrogation with a replacement is divided into:]

- stricture; and
- leniency.

It is possible for:

- the Quran to abrogate the Quran;
- the Quran to abrogate the Sunna; and
- the Sunna to abrogate the Sunna.

It is possible for mass-transmitted reports [*mutawātir*] to abrogate mass-transmitted reports, and for solitary reports and mass-transmitted reports to abrogate solitary reports [*āḥād*].

It is not possible for solitary reports to abrogate mass-transmitted reports.

CONFLICTING EVIDENCE

When two utterances conflict, it is inescapable that they are either

- both of universal applicability;
- both of particular applicability;
- one of them is universal and the other particular; or
- each one of them is universal from one perspective and particular from another.

If they are both of universal applicability and reconciliation is possible, they are reconciled.

If reconciliation between the conflicting evidence is not possible, then one must withhold judgment if their historical order is not known.

If their historical order is known, the previous is abrogated by the subsequent.

It is the same if they are both of particular applicability.

If one of the two texts is of universal applicability and the other is of particular applicability, the universal applicability [of one text] is restricted by the particular applicability [of the other text].

If each one of the two texts is of universal applicability from one aspect and of particular applicability from another, then the universal applicability of each one is restricted by the particular applicability of the other.

SCHOLARLY CONSENSUS

Scholarly consensus [*ijmaʿ*] is [when] the scholars of an era agree upon the ruling of an actual or potential issue. By "scholars" we mean the jurists [*fuqahā*]. By "new issue" we mean a new legal issue.

The Binding Legal Value of Consensus

The consensus of the Muslim community is binding [*ḥujja*] – but not that of other communities. This is because he ﷺ said, "My community will not come to consensus over a misguidance." The Legislation conveyed this community's protection.

Consensus is binding over the next generation, no matter in which generation it takes place.

In order for it to be binding, it is not a condition that the [entire] generation pass away.

If we were to say that the generation passing away is a condition, then the opinion of someone who was born during their lifetime, became a legist and qualified to make personal reasoning would be of consideration, and they are entitled to recant that ruling.

Consensus is valid by means of their words and their deeds. [Consensus is valid] by the statements and deeds of [just] some of them, when that statement or deed spreads while the remainder keeps silent.

The opinion of a single Companion (God be well pleased with them all) is not a binding proof over anyone else, according to [Imam al-Shāfiʿī's] new school.

DECLARATIVE STATEMENTS AND REPORTS

A declarative statement [*khabr*] is a statement wherein truth and falsehood enter.

Declarative statements are divided into solitary [*āḥād*] and mass-transmitted [*mutawātir*] reports.

Mass-Transmitted and Solitary Reports

Mass-transmitted [*mutawātir*] reports are those that necessarily convey sure knowledge [*'ilm*]. A mass-transmitted report is that which has been related by a group the likes of which cannot simultaneously agree upon a lie, from a similar group, [and so on,] up until the thing being reported; and the thing being reported being something observed or heard – not personal reasoning.

Solitary reports [*āḥād*] are those that necessarily lead to performance but do not necessarily convey sure knowledge [*'ilm*] because of bearing the possibility of it being a mistake.

Expedient and Grounded Reports

Reports divide into two divisions:

- expedient; and
- grounded.

Grounded reports [*musnad*] are those possessing a continuously connected chain of transmitters [*sanad*].

Expedient reports [*mursal*] are those lacking a continuously connected chain. If the expedient report is not from one of the Companions (God be well pleased with them), it is not a binding proof – unless it is an expedient report from Sa'īd bin al-Musayyab (May Allah be pleased with him), since his reports have been examined and grounded chains of transmission were found.

[Reports using] *indecisive hadith transmission* terminology [*'an'ana*] enter into grounded reports.

When the shaykh reads, it is permissible for the transmitter to say: "he related to me" [*ḥaddathanī*], or: "he informed me" [*akhbaranī*]. When he reads to the shaykh, he says: "he informed me," but does not say: "he related to me."

If the shaykh authorizes him without reading, the transmitter says: "he authorized me," or: "he informed me through an authorization."

ANALOGICAL REASONING

Analogical reasoning is returning a derived case [*far'*] back to the original case [*aṣl*] due to an apparent cause [*'illah*] that joins them in the ruling.

Divisions of Analogical Reasoning

Analogical reasoning divides into three divisions: *causative, indicative,* and *similitude.*

Causative analogy [*qiyās al-'illah*] is that in which the apparent cause [*'illah*] necessarily requires the ruling.

Indicative analogy [*qiyās al-dalālah*] is using one of two identical things as evidence for the other. It is when the apparent cause [*'illah*] indicates the ruling without necessarily requiring the ruling.

Analogy of similitude [*qiyās al-shabah*] is when the derived case resembles two source cases, so it is attached to whichever one it most resembles.

Conditions for the Integrals of Analogical Reasoning

A condition of the derived case is that it be appropriate to the original case.

A condition of the original case is that it is established through evidence that is agreed upon by the debating parties.

A condition of the apparent cause [*'illah*] is that it is constant in the rulings wherein it exists, so that it not be inconsistent in phrase or meaning.

A condition of the ruling [*ḥukm*] is that it be similar to the apparent cause [*'illah*] with regard to absence and presence.

The apparent cause [*'illah*] is what attracts the ruling, and the ruling is that which is attracted by the apparent cause.

PROHIBITION AND PERMISSIBILITY

As for impermissibility and permissibility: some scholars say that things are impermissible unless the Legislation declares it permissible. And so, if nothing in the Legislation is found that indicates permissibility, one adheres to the original state – impermissibility.

Some scholars hold the opposite: that the default state for things is the opposite [permissibility], except for what the Legislation has declared impermissible.

PRESUMPTION OF CONTINUITY

The meaning of "presumption of continuity" [*istiṣḥāb al-ḥāl*] is that the original state is presumed to continue in the absence of legal evidence.

THE ORDER OF PRECEDENCE IN WHICH EVIDENCE IS CITED

Manifest evidence is given precedence over the hidden.

Evidence that necessarily leads to sure knowledge [*'ilm*] is given precedence over evidence which leads to probable knowledge [*ẓann*].

Something stated is given precedence over analogical reasoning.

Manifest analogical reasoning [*qiyās jalī*] is given precedence over concealed analogical reasoning [*qiyās khafī*].

If something stated categorically is found to change the default state [it isused]. Otherwise the original state is presumed to continue [*istiṣḥāb al-ḥāl*].

THE MUFTI, HIS PETITIONER & EMULATION

The Muftī

Conditions of the *muftī* who is the *mujtahid* include

- being knowledgeable in *fiqh* – its foundations and branches – in the differences of opinion and the school's position;
- being versed in the tools necessary for *ijtihād* by knowing the tools that are needed to deduce rulings, including Arabic grammar and lexicography;
- being versed in narrators; and
- being versed in the commentaries of Quranic verses and Prophetic hadiths concerning rulings.

The Petitioner

A condition of the one petitioning the *muftī* [*al-mustaftī*] is being from those who imitate scholars, so he follows the *muftī* in his verdict.

It is not permissible for a scholar to imitate.

Imitating

Imitating [*taqlīd*] is accepting another's opinion without its proof. Consequently, accepting the opinion of the Prophet ﷺ is called "imitation."

Some said that imitation is to accept another's opinion while you do not know from where he took it.

If we hold the opinion that the Prophet (may Allah bless him and give him peace) gave rulings based on analogical reasoning, then it is permissible to call accepting his opinion imitation.

PERSONAL REASONING

Ijtihād ["personal reasoning"] is expending all efforts in reaching the goal. When a *mujtahid* exercises independent reasoning in branch issues and he has complete [mastery of the] tools for independent reasoning and he hits the mark – he has two rewards; if he exercises independent reasoning and misses then he has one.

It is not possible to hold the opinion that every *mujtahid* in root theological issues (beliefs) hits the mark since it would lead to declaring those who are misguided, Zoroastrians, non-believers, and atheists, as hitting the mark.

The evidence for those who say that every *mujtahid* does not [always] hit the mark is the saying of the Prophet ﷺ: "Whoever exercises independent reasoning and hits the mark gets two rewards, and whoever exercises independent reasoning and misses gets one reward." The reasoning is that the Prophet ﷺ declared some *mujtahid*s missing the mark sometimes, and declared them hitting it in others.

And God knows best.

BIBLIOGRAPHY

المصادر والمراجع

Al-Bukhārī, Muḥammad ibn Ismā'īl. *Ṣaḥīḥ al-Bukhārī.* Hadith numbering according to *Fatḥ al-Bārī.*

Al-Dimyāṭī, Aḥmed bin Muḥammad, Jalāl al-Dīn al-Maḥallī, al-Juwaynī. *Ḥāshiyat 'alā Sharḥ al-Waraqāt.* Cairo: 'Abd al-Ḥamīd Aḥmad Ḥanafī, 1370AH.

Al-Ḥākim, Abū 'Abdallāh. *Al-Mustadrak 'alā al-Ṣaḥīḥayn.* 4 vols. Hyderabad, 1334AH/1916CE. Reprint (with index vol 5). Beirut: Dār al-Ma'rifah, n.d.

Ibn Ḥanbal, Aḥmad. *Al-Musnad.* 6 vols. Cairo: Mu'assasat Qurṭuba, n.d. Reprint. Beirut: Dār Iḥyā' al-Turāth al-'Arabī, n.d.

Ibn Mājah, Muḥammad. *Sunan Ibn Mājah.* Edited by Fu'ād 'Abd al-Bāqī. 2 vols. Beirut: Dār al-Fikr, n.d.

Al-Jāwī, Aḥmad bin 'Abd al-Khaṭīb, Jalāl al-Dīn al-Maḥallī, al-Juwaynī. *Ḥāshiyat al-Nafaḥāt 'alā Sharḥ al-Waraqāt.* Cairo: Muṣṭafā al-Bābī al-Ḥalabī, 1357AH/1937CE.

Al-Juwaynī, 'Abd al-Malak, Ibn al-Firkāḥ. *Sharḥ al-Waraqāt.* Edited and annotated by Sārah Shāfī al-Hājarī. Beirut: Dār al-Bashā'ir al-Islāmiyyah, 1423AH/2001CE.

——, Jalāl al-Dīn al-Maḥallī. *Sharḥ Matn al-Waraqāt.* Edited and annotated by 'Abd al-Salām al-Shannār. Damascus: n.a., n.d.

——, Jalāl al-Dīn al-Maḥallī, Ibn Qāsim al-'Ubādī. *Sharḥ 'alā Sharḥ al-Waraqāt.* Printed in the margins of Muḥmammad bin 'Alī al-Shawkānī's *Irshād al-Fuḥūl.* Beirut: Dār al-Ma'rifah, n.d.

Muslim ibn al-Ḥajjāj. *Ṣaḥīḥ Muslim.* Edited by Muḥammad Fu'ād 'Abd al-Bāqī. 5 vols. Cairo: Maṭba'ah 'Īsā al-Bābī al-Ḥalabī 1376AH/1956CE. Reprint. Beirut: Dār al-Fikr, 1403 AH/1983CE.

Al-Nasā'ī, Abū 'Abd al-Raḥmān Aḥmad. *Al-Sunan al-Kubrā*. Beirut: Dār Iḥyā' al-Turāth al-'Arabī, n.d.

Al-Sajistānī, Abū Dāwūd. *Sunan Abī Dāwūd*. Edited by Muḥammad Muḥyī al-Dīn 'Abd al-Ḥamīd. 4 vols. in 2. Beirut: Dār al-Fikr, n.d.

Al-Tirmidhī, Abū 'Īsā. *Sunan al-Tirmidhī*. Edited by Muḥammad Fu'ād 'Abd al-Bāqī. 5 vols. Cairo, n.d. Reprint. Beirut: Dār Iḥyā' al-Turāth al-'Arabī, n.d.

CPSIA information can be obtained
at www.ICGtesting.com
Printed in the USA
BVOW03s0033281217
503816BV00001BA/30/P

9 780985 884048